To all the members of the cooking club, who have taught me about dovering and biscuit beaters, oysters and angel food cake. This book is for home cooking and all the home cooks who came before us, and I can't wait to taste what comes next.

Copyright ©2018 by MM BOOKWORKS, LLC.

Printed by Donlevy Lithograph, Wichita, Kansas

Published by MM BOOKWORKS, LLC.
9131 E Autumn Chase Street
Wichita, Kansas 67206

All rights reserved. No part of this book may be reproduced in any form or by any electronic or mechanical means, including information storage and retrieval systems, without permission in writing from the publisher, except by a reviewer who may quote brief passages in a review.

First edition

ISBN 978-0-9966201-1-6

Edited by Julia Langel, Ph.D., and Everett Langel

Research and writing by Sondra Langel

Design by Greteman Group

Photography by Larry Schwarm

Available at ThursdayAfternoonCookingClub.com

CONTENTS

- 6   ACKNOWLEDGMENTS
- 8   FOREWORD BY ERIC CALE

THURSDAY AFTERNOON COOKING CLUB
- 10   THE ART OF COOKING
- 18   EARLY DAYS OF THE COOKING CLUB
- 28   THE 20TH CENTURY BEGINS
- 40   WORLD WAR COMES TO AMERICA
- 66   AMERICAN COOKING 1960 – 2018

LUNCHEON MENUS
- 76   TASTES OF THE MEDITERRANEAN
- 88   MID-CENTURY REVISITED
- 94   COOL AND CASUAL
- 102   MAKING MEMORIES
- 110   CLASSIC CUISINE
- 120   HEARTY FALL FEAST
- 128   IN THE TEX-MEX STYLE
- 138   LADIES' BRIDGE LUNCHEON
- 148   CHRISTMAS LUNCHEON
- 158   ITALIAN PRANZO
- 166   A FAMILY AFFAIR
- 174   FEASTING WITH FLAIR
- 182   KANSAS DINNER
- 190   EASY ELEGANCE
- 198   125TH ANNIVERSARY CELEBRATION
- 208   TINY TREASURES, POTS DE CRÈME
- 226   INDEX

ACKNOWLEDGMENTS

One of my favorite mystery writers likes to start his acknowledgements with "I did this all myself." Much as I love the humor of it, in my case it just wouldn't work. There was this whole club of helpful women doing whatever they could to make this book informative and true and historic and also new.

The Thursday Afternoon Cooking Club took a leap of faith when they authorized Larry Schwarm and me to do this book, mostly on the basis of our previous publication of *Wichita Artists in Their Studios*. We promised to team up with the same crew who produced our first book, and the Greteman Group signed up very quickly and has been diligently moving us along in this new endeavor.

The club turned over to us its treasures: many, many years of minutes, mostly handwritten, photos and clippings in scrapbooks, recipes, and a list of their favorite menus for us to choose among. Their current president, Barb Mohney, helped whenever she could, and Rebecca Ritchey served as our liaison with the club members.

But that's not all. A cooking book needs recipes that are tested and tested again, so I declared my kitchen a testing kitchen for a month. Members of the club showed up in a daily rotation, wore aprons and gloves and tested every recipe we were considering.

They chatted as they cooked, and stories arose that were eventually used in the book. These women are a delightful group to chop peppers and onions with.

Larry Schwarm has been my partner in two publications and my good friend as well. His eye for a good photo makes this book glow with yummy-looking food, much of which we ate together after the photos were done.

This year Adriene Rathbun joined the team as food stylist – the person who arranges the chives on top, as someone once characterized styling. More than that, of course, she knew how backgrounds and dishes would affect the appearance of food.

For layout, the Greteman Group has been our salvation. They understand our wish for a beautiful book, yet one that teaches and instructs. Combining a 127-year-long club and food history with a cooking book was tricky, but they are the masters of maximizing type and photography.

And again, Julia Langel has been strict with her mother by editing pieces out and in all through the process. Everett Langel, I suspect, loved being asked to proofread and find all my mistakes in typing, etc. My helper, Joanie Allenbach, has been available whenever needed. They all kept me on the job when daily living threatened to derail the whole operation.

Because food history was a new subject for me, I consulted a number of sources, including but not limited to the names below.

Sondra Langel

A FOOD LOVER'S COMPANION
EVAN JONES

A HISTORY OF FOOD IN 100 RECIPES
WILLIAM SITWELL

BOSTON COOKING SCHOOL COOKBOOK
FANNIE MERRITT FARMER

CONSIDER THE FORK
BEE WILSON

FOOD IN HISTORY
REAY TANNAHILL

FRESH AND SOPHISTICATED
CLAIRE MAGUIRE

NEWSPAPERS.COM

MONDAY MORNING COOKING CLUB
THE MONDAY MORNING COOKING CLUB

PERFECTION SALAD
LAURA SHAPIRO

PINCHES AND DASHES
THE JUNIOR LEAGUE OF WICHITA

SOMETHING FROM THE OVEN
LAURA SHAPIRO

THE AMERICAN PASTRY COOK
JESSUP WHITEHEAD

THE MIDDLE EASTERN KITCHEN
RUKMINI IYER

WICHITA CENTURY
R.M. "DICK" LONG

WOMEN OF GREAT TASTE
THE JUNIOR LEAGUE OF WICHITA

FOREWORD
BY ERIC CALE
DIRECTOR, WICHITA-SEDGWICK COUNTY HISTORICAL MUSEUM

Wichita is obsessed with Wichita. Wichitans have been fixated on their history from the moment they started making it, and no one seems more fascinated with the place lately than its young people who carry astonishing enthusiasm for this city, considered by outsiders to be only somewhere to fly over, if anything at all. Wichitans are possessed of a pride of place that is, at least in part, a recognition of earlier citizens' creative response to unique challenges. These included geographical remoteness; the vast, seemingly vacant barrenness of the prairie; and the unencumbered, undefined nature of a locale so recently settled. This attitude also comes from the tendency for the "self-talk" necessary to navigate uncharted territory.

The unusual history that gave rise to Wichita also helps to explain this spirit. The city's first newspaper, the *Wichita Vidette*, published in 1870, devoted considerable print to local history in its first issue. Subsequent official historical sketches continued the tradition of reporting local history, but glossed over certain past events. These histories typically began with the Spanish conquistadors, segued to French explorers and colorful trappers, but typically ignored Native Americans who were too little understood to appear as anything except an obstacle to settlement.

Here's a more factual encapsulation of Wichita's history: In 1861 when the Civil War began and eleven states left the Union, Kansas joined the Union as a free state situated front and center of the country's frontier and its westward expansion. Wichita did not exist then; the area was in fact the land of the Osage, Kiowa and other native tribes and was not open to settlement.

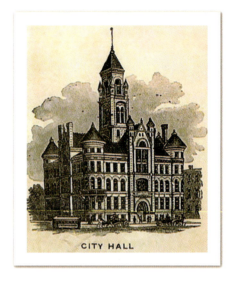
CITY HALL

Months after the Civil War's end in 1865, Native Americans relinquished their claim through a treaty recorded as number 342. Within five years the city of Wichita was incorporated in the county of Sedgwick, also established that year and named for the Union hero famous for his last words at the Battle of Spotsylvania, "They couldn't hit an elephant at this distance." Wichita, situated in the narrow Arkansas (pronounced "R-Kansas") River Valley, came to be the West's primary post-war destination. Within two decades it would become the fastest-growing city in the United States.

This new city attracted the adventurous, the creative and the enterprising. The late 19th century was a time of advances in areas such as electrical power, transportation, communication, medical technology, education, social justice and public services. These coupled with established American ideals suggested a masterpiece could be created on this blank canvas in the Great American Desert. As these forces gathered, self-improvement and a higher standard of living (including the realization of leisure time) became a common goal.

Women's roles were expanding and especially unbridled on the frontier. Famously, Olive Ann Beech, leader of Beech Aircraft, and Louise Brooks, the definitive screen actress of the 1920s, stand out in the pantheon of notable Wichita women. Their archetypal precedent might be Catherine McCarty (mother of the notorious outlaw "Billy the Kid"), the lone woman to sign the city's charter. She had the right to own property including a farm and the city laundry, but the right to vote was still 42 years in her future (in Kansas the vote came in 1912, eight years before national suffrage in 1920). Lucetta Carter was a noted businesswoman and philanthropist who helped establish the Unitarian Church and promoted wider access to literature. The sagacity of local women is further reflected in the formation of local women's clubs. Mary Elizabeth Lease was active as an advocate of women's suffrage, the temperance movement and the liberally inclusive Populist Party. Lease founded the Hypatia Club in 1886 to empower and widen women's awareness of their roles in society. Wichitan Jane Brooks rose to national prominence in the fight for women's suffrage and eventually established the Sedgwick County League of Women Voters, the first local league in the United States. Louise Caldwell Murdock, founder of the 20th Century Club in 1899, is notable for instilling cultural arts in the city's consciousness. She, like McCarty, was a business owner paving the way for other enterprising Wichita women, such as young and single June Frisby who, beginning in the 1920s, owned and operated a major music studio, educating generations of students, or Xavia Hightower, funeral director and successful civil rights activist whose Cadillac's custom license plate read "Lady Mortician." Forward thinking was standard Wichita thinking.

The city's boom in manufacturing began with the production and distribution of farming equipment and tractors, followed by the production of aircraft. This later reached its zenith during World War II when the city operated "24-7" to produce the B-29 Bomber used to win the war. Wichita also became a notable seed bed for modern food service concepts. Concurrent with the rise of Wichita's aviation industry came the genesis of fast food, with White Castle, America's first fast-food chain, opening downtown in 1921. White Castle encouraged husbands to give their wives a night off from cooking each week by buying a bag of burgers. The franchise attempted to convince the public that their facility and methods were healthful and sanitary by dressing employees in white outfits associated with the medical profession. About forty years later another franchising masterstroke materialized with the emergence of Pizza Hut, at about the same time Wichita's William Lear introduced private jet airplanes to the world.

Today the city is known for building upon these accomplishments and for its ability to survive on its own terms, transcending national turmoil, economic and otherwise. The city's culture has evolved to suit its inhabitants and has not been over-engineered to mimic trends and impress outsiders. In 150 years the city's style and culture have taken shape and achieved definition. It can ironically be interpreted as a place of steady predictability and yet a place where anything might happen.

1

THE ART OF COOKING

The enduring story of the Thursday Afternoon Cooking Club began in the Fall of 1891, when Mrs. E.R. Spangler (Laura) of Wichita, Kansas, sent a note to a few of her friends inviting them to join her in creating a cooking club. This was not to be a social club. It had as its purpose an exchange of ideas about the art of cooking and domestic science. Mrs. Spangler was a cooking teacher. She taught a class for teenagers, and one of her special concerns was that young women did not know how to entertain. She also worried that many married women depended entirely on servants for recipes and "dainty" dishes, as she called them.

THE PURSUIT OF CULINARY ART

Laura Spangler wanted a club dedicated to the pursuit of knowledge of the culinary art, and she was looking for friends with whom she could engage.

Amazingly enough, this club has persevered more than 127 years as a bimonthly and then later, a monthly gathering. The members have retained handwritten minutes, newspaper clippings and photos, and gained high recognition amongst women's clubs for their longevity and accomplishments. These minutes and clippings have made it possible to reconstruct their long history seen through their eyes.

And also, it must be said, through the eyes of the author of this book, a nonmember of the club, and a person fascinated as much by the history as by the food. Telling the story involves more than the somewhat stilted minutes written in old log books. Placing their actions into the temper and tempo of the times required delving into resources of many styles, some of them online, and others in books and even conversation. This is a Kansas club, and Kansas was caught up in the strife and struggle, economic and political, at the end of the 19th century.

Increasing industrialization made household staffing expensive and more difficult to attract. At the same time, wealthier homes were still expected to produce lavish meals of delicacies meant to impress guests for weddings and other important social events. Married ladies needed to be self-sufficient and resourceful. Learning to cook was more and more important.

THE NEW FOOD SCIENCE

During the last decade of the 19th century, industrialization had changed home life as well as working life. With it had come new inventions: gas and electricity, the typewriter, the telephone, the light bulb, the calorie. Thoughtful women – homemakers – were beginning to see a link between the new science and their own lives. A major movement called "domestic reform" was happening. They were learning how germs and lack of nutrition could lead directly to social miseries, and this was serious stuff.

The Wichita women who started the cooking club were on the front edge of the new food science.

ORGANIZING A COOKING CLUB

At their first meeting they elected a president, Mrs. Spangler, a secretary and a treasurer.

Each meeting was to be a luncheon prepared by members according to a schedule set out at the beginning of each year. Members in groups of three would hold meetings in the home of one of the hostesses. Cooking demonstrations and new equipment were to be a highlight in order to increase culinary knowledge and technique. Every menu needed to be perfect. The original members voted to have dishes prepared before them for "the pleasure of tasting and criticizing them."

MEMBERSHIP

The original membership was selected by Mrs. Spangler. Later, members needed to be proposed in writing, and voted upon by the membership. As the years went by, it seemed appropriate to add daughters, daughters-in-law, granddaughters and even great granddaughters. Today at least half of the current members trace their membership to a previous relative.

At its second meeting in 1891, the club adopted the motto "Health, Strength, Happiness" and the colors of green and yellow. They also decided to name the club The Thursday Afternoon Cooking Club (TACC). They agreed that the only acceptable excuses for nonattendance were illness or being out of town. TACC members did not, and do not, miss meetings.

Although Mrs. Spangler was the originator, the acknowledged "mother" of the club was Mrs. B.H. Campbell (Ellen) who served as president for eleven years, from 1896 to 1907. She is credited with giving the time, strength and advice that prepared the club for its phenomenal survival. Mrs. Campbell became a driving force behind important club activities, including the publishing of small cookbooks with practical recipes and housekeeping hints. She was an accomplished cook, and contributed many recipes to the club's cookbooks, big and small.

LEADERSHIP

The current club president is Mrs. Rich Mohney (Barb), the great granddaughter of Mrs. B.H. Campbell. Barb's warmth and humor punctuate club meetings, and set a relaxed and informal atmosphere. Barb is the third generation of the Campbell family to be a member of the club. She follows her relatives, Mrs. B.H. Campbell, Mrs. Alfred M. Campbell and Mrs. H.G. Norton.

Some Choice Receipts

When the club published a cookbook called "Some Choice Receipts," paid for by the Union Mill Company, a Wichita flour producer, Ellen Campbell wrote the introduction. In it she sets out her belief in the importance of cooking. " . . . a well-baked bread, good, broiled, juicy steak, and a fine fragrant cup of coffee will materially lessen the patronage of the saloons and the divorce courts."

DINNER AT THE CASTLE

During its first year, the club presented a dinner for husbands held in Mrs. B.H. Campbell's home. Frequently known as Campbell Castle, it was modeled after a feudal Scottish castle, built with eight fireplaces, and includes a castellated tower with carved stone animal figures. The castle now serves Wichita as a bed and breakfast.

Mrs. Campbell's husband was Colonel B.H. "Barbecue" Campbell, an experienced rancher and breeder in Wichita. He was hired by the Texas legislature to manage a 3-million-acre ranch known as the XIT. In one year XIT employed 150 cowboys, who branded 35,000 calves. In 1888, rumors of gambling, alcohol and possible outlaws on the range resulted in his return to Wichita.

Secretary's Minutes, May 19, 1892 The ladies of the Cooking Club will long remember the banquet given at the palatial home of Mrs. B.H. Campbell. The large parlors and halls were well filled with warmly chatting guests early in the afternoon – at about 5:00 o'clock each member escorted her guest to their places at the banquet table, which extended the length of the library and dining room. Decorated as they were with dainty doilies, rare china, pretty silverware and flowers, the tables presented a most beautiful picture. Seven delicate and delicious courses were served.

Some Choice Receipts included an introduction written by Ellen Campbell.

***The Wichita Daily Eagle*, May 22, 1892,** carried a story about that Thursday Afternoon Cooking Club event. "Riverside never looked prettier than now, and as carriage after carriage pulled up to the porte cochere depositing their load of beautifully dressed ladies, who with smiling appreciation of the hospitable welcome of the massive portal, pressed on into the elegant interior. Many were the guesses made as to which member of the club furnished the various articles on the sumptuous menu."

Mrs. B.H. Campbell, above, was the great grandmother of current club president, Mrs. Rich Mohney (Barb), below.

Secretary's Minutes, May 24, 1892 A business meeting was held for the purpose of settling accounts for the banquet. Dues collected were $7.60. Members having two guests at the banquet were taxed $.40. It was voted that the next menu consist of Cake and Cream all donated by members so as to pay the remaining debt.

COMPLETE MENUS FOR LUNCHEONS

In addition to telling the story of the club, this book presents a wide variety of recipes in the context of carefully planned menus. Menu crafting provides a party-ready head start for anyone looking for entertaining ideas. TACC invites you to follow their lead. They have selected these menus from the thousands accumulated over the years. They do not pretend to have invented the recipes, but have borrowed from their grandmothers' files, favorite cookbooks, and online postings and identify the source whenever possible. Each menu was tested, critiqued and retested. This can save you work, but you can, of course, pick and choose to create your own menus.

Every recipe was presented for a club luncheon, and each dish received an after-lunch critique from the members. In preparation for this book, members participated in a month-long testing kitchen, checking every recipe. The book's author and food stylist tested each recipe again while photographing the food.

The Thursday Afternoon Cooking Club hopes you will find in this book the stories, affection, laughter and learning that make this club worthwhile. Putting together the book prompted remembering good things to eat and good moments of companionship. Now the club hopes to share them with you.

Mrs. Ralph Millison, Nettie Fitch, Mrs. George Dickson, Mrs. B.H. Campbell getting ready to teach a cooking class.

2

EARLY DAYS OF THE COOKING CLUB

By 1886 wheat had supplanted cattle as the major force in the Wichita economy. The city now had streets and even streetlights. Mennonite settlers arriving from Russia who were accustomed to growing wheat in a prairie climate found success with wheat in Kansas and encouraged other farmers to plant it here. Mennonite families loaded kitchen crocks and traveling trunks with hard winter wheat seed before leaving Russia.

Secretary's Minutes, February 4, 1894
Motion to the effect that we wear white aprons during our meetings as a club. Made and carried.

BEYOND WICHITA'S COWTOWN ORIGINS

In 1891, only twenty years old as a city, Wichita's citizens wanted it to move beyond its cowtown origins. Kansas was already being called "The Wheat State" and "The Breadbasket of The World." But along came a severe drought, and together with the rest of the nation, Kansas suffered a huge depression. Farms failed, and the whole country was affected by strikes of railroad workers, miners and even newsboys. William Jennings Bryan, a populist and Democrat, ran for U. S. president. The populist movement resonated strongly with the "Free-State" independence of Kansans.

HYPATIA CLUB

The Populist Party became a major force in Wichita with the arrival of Mary Elizabeth Lease. Built on a coalition of poor, white cotton farmers and hard-pressed wheat farmers in the Plains states (especially Kansas and Nebraska), the Populist Party represented a radical crusading form of agrarianism and hostility to elites, cities, banks, railroads and gold. Mrs. Lease was a powerful and emotional speaker; Emporia, Kansas editor William Allen White, who did not share her political views, wrote on one occasion that "she could recite the multiplication table and set a crowd hooting and harrahing at her will." Mrs. Lease formed the Hypatia Club in Wichita. Hypatia's goal was "to promote good fellowship and happiness and strive for our cultural enlightenment." She put an ad in *The Wichita Eagle* inviting intelligent women, artists, musicians, teachers, actors, lecturers, and all women having the advancement of their sex in view, to meet with her. The Eagle's editor, Marshall Murdock, wrote an editorial urging husbands to keep their wives at home. The idea was simply unheard of in a Victorian society in which women catered to their men and, at best, only met to exchange recipes and for quilting bees. Mrs. Lease wanted more for women.

PROGRESS FOR WOMEN

It was within this framework of politics and the ragged economy that Mrs. Spangler decided to start the Thursday Afternoon Cooking Club. Laura Spangler was not a free-all-day society lady. She was a working woman. She owned a cooking school for young ladies, including teens, and also helped promote new ranges and special hardware for cooking. She joined the Hypatia Club, so we may assume she was politically active in the early struggle for women's rights. She served the Thursday Afternoon Cooking Club until 1905, when she moved with her husband to California.

Another early member of TACC was Mrs. Lorenzo Lewelling (Ida), the wife of the governor of Kansas, who was elected in 1893 on the Populist ticket in the most turbulent election ever held in Kansas. It involved armed militias confronting congressional gatherings. After his term as governor, Ida and her husband, active abolitionists, returned to Wichita where they pursued numerous business opportunities, mostly in the banking and loan sector.

AN ENDURING RECORD

The first TACC secretary, Mrs. C.J. Fletcher, found a ledger originally used for minutes of the city hospital, and began recording minutes for every meeting. That precious ledger survives today as part of the history of the club. It and minute books from ensuing years have been primary sources for tracing the history of the club.

MINUTES

We learn a great deal about activities of the club from those early minutes. They were at first very businesslike. At meetings, the secretary read the minutes and the treasurer told the balance on the books, as well as who had and not paid dues. Large portions of the meetings were given over to reading out recipes so that members could write them down. They also shared household hints. Organizing future meetings and menus consumed every session.

MEETINGS

The earliest members of the club were married to prominent businessmen in a striving and burgeoning new city. They lived in the best sections. A few of their homes still remain, although most have been replaced or drastically remodeled. Their structures were very different from what people need today. Because cooking was done on a wood or coal stove and frequently accomplished only by cooking staff, the kitchens were frequently located on a lower level or sometimes outside the house to manage the heat and possibility of fire. Style was important, and beautiful dishes and glassware were treasured. The earliest minutes of the club do not mention details about table settings except to remark on the beauty of the day and the general loveliness of the event. Later on, the minutes lavished great praise on flower arrangements.

Invitations were not sent out. The club relied on a printed notice in the local newspaper *The Wichita Daily Beacon* about the time and location of the next meeting. The meeting was usually followed by a newspaper review of the menu and guests present.

Telephones were not available in homes until well after the turn of the century. These ladies attended meetings and made their "calls" by riding in a horse-drawn carriage or walking. There were typewriters, of course, but they relied on handwriting for menus, receipts, notes and recording minutes.

ANGEL FOOD CAKE
THE FIRST COOKING DEMONSTRATION

From the original ledger, we know that the first real cooking meeting was December 31, 1891, in the home of Mrs. Fletcher. Her husband operated a grocery store on North Main Street. An 1890 ad for his store advertised 15 lbs. of sugar for $1.

For this meeting, Mrs. Rush had been appointed to demonstrate making an angel food cake. It was a complete success, and has been a popular dessert during all the years of the club. The minutes tell us that two salad dressings were made from the egg yolks left over from the cake, and were used in lobster and chicken salads " . . . to test their delicacy. Both were delicious."

To appreciate the cake, one must think about what baking was like in those early days. The structure depends on lots of air beaten into egg whites. In the 1890s it was probably beaten for a very long time with a wire whisk. The science of beating volume into foods was not well known at that time.

Cooks carefully sifted and re-sifted, measured and re-measured flour and sugar into a big earthenware bowl and worked for an hour or more beating the egg whites by hand. They poured the batter carefully into an ungreased pan with a round center post because the cake needed to cling to all sides in order to rise to the desired very high level.

Someone needed to load wood or coal into the firebox and light the flames. The cook would have to test by hand how hot the oven seemed. These ovens did not have thermometers, so placing this delicate cake into that uncertain environment defies common sense. But they did it, and they celebrated the amazing creation they made.

AN AMERICAN INVENTION

Angel food cake was a perfect choice for the very first baking demonstration at the cooking club. It was a recent American invention, called "the food of angels" because of its light and fluffy texture and sweet taste. It was very special and hard to make, and precisely the right way for the new club to begin learning cooking techniques.

In *The American Pastry Cook,* 1894, author Jessup Whitehead claimed the cake was invented in 1878 by S. Sides, who had a restaurant in St. Louis where he served this elegant dessert. It became so popular he had orders from as far away as London. "For some time the method of making it was kept a profound secret, but at length the inventor yielded so far as to sell his recipe for $25, having it understood that it could not be made without a certain powder that could be obtained from him alone. It did not take long to discover that the powder was nothing but cream of tartar, and the recipe became common property."

Baking this sweet delicacy engendered a real sense of achievement for women who may have been relying on servants to do their cooking. There is a sense of mystique about its fluffy height and springy texture.

Making the cake from scratch has become a badge of honor for members. A handwritten recipe by honorary member Roberta (Bert) Feibach has been used by members since the 1960s for producing this high-volume, light-as-air delicacy. Her cakes became the gold standard, even as members quietly later agreed that a good box mix works very well.

MOM'S ANGEL FOOD
(BERT FEIBACH) WITH CHOCOLATE WHIPPED CREAM ICING

1 C + 2 T CAKE FLOUR
¾ C SUGAR
1 C SIFTED SUGAR
1½ CUPS EGG WHITES
½ TSP SALT
1½ TSP CREAM OF TARTAR
1 TSP VANILLA
½ TSP ALMOND FLAVORING

FOR CHOCOLATE ANGEL FOOD
SUBSTITUTE ¼ C COCOA FOR ¼ C FLOUR AND SIFT AS IN FIRST STEP

MARILYN WELLS CHOCOLATE ICING
½ C POWDERED SUGAR
3 LEVEL T DROSTE'S IMPORTED COCOA
1 PINT HEAVY WHIPPING CREAM
1 TSP VANILLA

Angel Food Oven 375°F. Sift together five times: 1 cup + 2 tablespoons cake flour, ¾ cups sugar. For chocolate angel food: Substitute ¼ cup cocoa for ¼ cup flour and sift as in first step. Have ready: 1 cup sifted sugar. In large bowl beat until foamy (or try beating eggs longer): 1½ cups egg whites (let cups run over), ½ teaspoon salt. Add 1½ teaspoons cream of tartar. Continue beating only until when you lift up beaters it will peak and then flop over (only 2-3 minutes). Circle bowl slowly with beaters. Sprinkle in gradually the 1 cup sifted sugar about 3 tablespoons at a time rounded. Use wire whip for this: fold only until sugar is blended. Add this after sugar is folded in: 1 teaspoon vanilla, ½ teaspoon almond flavoring. Add flour mixture evenly and quickly (about 3 minutes). Fold with whip only enough to blend. Pour into tube pan. Cut the batter with a knife. Bake 30 minutes (or less in Teflon). May need to be set higher to brown cake. Check by pressing top with finger. Invert until cool.

Chocolate Whipped Cream Icing Sift powdered sugar and cocoa. Stir this into a bowl of unwhipped cream. Let set in refrigerator 1½ hours. Remove and whip. Add vanilla. Slice angel food cake in half horizontally. Spread icing on cut layer. Replace the top layer and frost top and sides of cake. Chill 12 hours before serving.

Marilyn Wells

Since angel food has become a regular offering from TACC members over the years, Marilyn Wells, currently the longest-serving member, volunteered to demonstrate how to frost an angel food cake using her special recipe. Marilyn insists that the Dutch chocolate (Droste) is the only correct choice for this chocolate icing. Helping Marilyn is her daughter Anne Allen, who happens to be the youngest current TACC member.

TACC AND TECHNOLOGY

The 1890s were a dizzying time for new discoveries. The "Ladies Phaeton" in 1893 was the first commercially manufactured automobile. Thomas Edison and William Dickson invented and developed the Kinetoscope, a motion picture device. The zipper, electric kettle, typewriter, aspirin, cold cereal, Cracker Jack, Hershey Chocolate Bar, jukebox, escalator and Shredded Wheat were all encompassed in the development frenzy, as were the fountain pen and golf tee.

The women wanted to know about all these new things, particularly as they related to home life. They were curious, and every meeting was designed to introduce them to new tools or procedures. New recipes were always important, but they wanted new technologies as well.

PEERLESS STEAM COOKER

The steam cooker is huge. It stands nearly two feet high and is 14 inches across. Used for cooking vegetables and meat and for preserving fruit.

BEATEN BISCUIT MACHINE

A table-style beaten biscuit brake was used for rolling dough to make old fashioned layered biscuits. Beaten biscuits are denser and harder than traditional soft or buttermilk biscuits, and they don't crumble like a "normal" biscuit. They actually are closely related to hardtack, associated with the Civil War. A version of beaten biscuits is also made in the American northeast to eat with – and often float in – chowders, like homemade oyster crackers. Originally, biscuits were beaten with wooden boards, folded and beaten again to make layers. The Biscuit Brake made the process easier. The dough was folded and sent repeatedly through the rollers.

THE DOVER EGG BEATER

The Dover beater was so popular that whipping became known in some circles as "dovering." In 1922, when the club published a hardcover cookbook, many recipes instructed cooks to "dover" the dish being made.

Secretary's Minutes, October 27, 1892 Before the meeting was called to order, our hostess introduced Mr. Edwards, who has for sale the Peerless Steam Cooker. I am sure the demonstration convinced the ladies present that the cooker would be a great convenience in their kitchens.

The Peerless Steam Cooker. Made in 1896.

Secretary's Minutes, February 1892 The Beaten Biscuit Machine, sometimes called Beaten Biscuit Brake, was introduced to the Club. The Beaten Biscuit Machine was quite a novel feature – each lady being given an opportunity to test her strength by turning the machine, which furnished quite a little sport for meeting members. . . . The biscuits were a grand success.

Beaten Biscuit Machine, circa 1900.

Secretary's Minutes, January 12, 1893 A gentleman came to the meeting trying to sell his cream and egg whipper machine, and added to the spirits of the members. . . . Mr. Egg Whipper Man, with the aid of an assistant, prepared the ice cream for dessert. . . . When everything was ready we sat down to the dining table where all enjoyed the feast of good things, as was attested by the merriment and repartee of the ladies.

The Dover Egg Beater. Made in 1891.

***The Wichita Beacon*, October, 12, 1893**
Mrs. E.R Spangler, the club's first president, was well-known for her Wichita Cooking School. The ad to the right features her "Celebrated Cooking School Bread."

Celebrated Corn Bread

Secretary's Minutes, January 27, 1893
Mrs. Baldwin brought her recipe for Stacked Pie, which had been served at the previous meeting to great acclaim.

***The Wichita Beacon*, October 25, 1895**
An article, called "They Cook," mentions the club enjoying cooking demonstrations and touts a delicious dessert made with "instantaneous" tapioca.

TACC LUNCHEONS BEGIN

Two years on, the club was functioning with meetings twice a month. They became regular meals, even though still punctuated with cooking and cookware demonstrations. The luncheons always included elaborate relish plates, a variety of salads (very often Tomato Aspic made the traditional way, by boiling bones to make a gel), a main course (usually some sort of oyster dish), bread or rolls, and remarkably elaborate desserts. The local newspapers published events of the Cooking Club in their social sections after almost every meeting. The following article mentioned "newly manufactured flour" for making angel food cakes. This was a low protein flour made from soft winter wheat, which gives it a very fine texture and a very light color. The article also mentions making ice cream using Rennet or Junket tablets.

STACKED PIE

In early days, when people went visiting, they brought food, and needed something that traveled well. Stacking three to five pies of different fillings and holding them together with a thin layer of icing was an answer. Very thin slices were served. Many stacked pies included chess pies because they are easy to make with a few ingredients, but any kind of pie could be made to "stack up."

CELEBRATED CORN BREAD

The stove pictured may have been very similar to the one Mrs. Spangler used, an 1890 Born Steel Range, to bake her bread. It is hard to imagine cooking on a wood stove. Early recipes did not include baking temperatures because there were no thermostats in those stoves. Cooking over wood or coals required a measure of physical labor both in loading them into the oven, and also cleaning out the unit. Unfortunately, we do not have the recipe for the Celebrated Corn Bread and we are left wondering why it was so celebrated. However, there was a recipe for Delicious Corn Bread, attributed to "Cooking School" in the small cookbook, *Choice Receipts*, the club produced in 1902. We can speculate this may have been the "celebrated" recipe.

DELICIOUS CORN BREAD

1 PT COOKED HOMINY GRITS, COOKED AS DRY AS POSSIBLE
1 PT SWEET MILK
½ PT CORN MEAL
1 T BUTTER
3 TSP BAKING POWDER
4 EGGS

Cook grits, add butter, beat in eggs one at a time; add meal, milk and baking powder. Heat skillet very hot; grease it and pour in the mixture. Bake in oven 20 minutes.

Cooking Club Dinner Party, circa 1905.

3

THE 20TH CENTURY BEGINS

In addition to teaching one another, members of the club were busy teaching cooking classes. They sponsored a junior cooking club, and once again cooperated with a milling company to produce a small cookbook entitled *Practical Recipes*. Giving in to changing terminology, they began using "recipes" instead of "receipts."

Secretary's Minutes, 1894 – 1910 Sadly, no TACC minute book for the period between 1894 and 1910 has survived. This wonderful photo, saved in a scrapbook, shows that there was a party with the husbands, held at the home of Mr. and Mrs. Findlay Ross (Ella), sometime around 1905. The home, sometimes called a mansion, was built in 1887 by William Henry Sternberg, a leading designer and builder of fine homes, especially in New York. Mr. Ross was a prominent businessman and later Wichita mayor, during which time he established Riverside Park.

PRACTICAL RECIPES

Practical Recipes included many recipes for oysters, a common food choice in those days. Oysters were extremely plentiful and inexpensive along the coasts of America, and railways carried thousands of barrels to Chicago for transport. Laid down in brine, live oysters were easily and cheaply brought to Wichita.

Practical Recipes contained recipes for oyster pot roast, oyster chops hollandaise, oyster bullion and escalloped oysters. All of these dishes were served at club luncheons.

WICHITA CAKE

Most especially, *Practical Recipes* included a recipe for a delicacy called "Wichita Cake," by Mrs. B.H. Campbell. This cake, when served to the club, April 21, 1892, was so extraordinary that a decision was made to send a piece to the editor of *The Wichita Eagle*. This recipe from 1905 translates very well to tastes of today. Because the Wichita Cake recipe came without directions – as do most old recipes – instructions have been added.

THE RISE OF HOME ECONOMICS

The rise of food science as a profession was a very big deal for young women at the turn of the century. Among other things, it gave them the opportunity to be a part of science – previously a realm open only to men.

In college, women studied the science of cookery and applied their knowledge to improving the nutrition and health of their families. Some became social workers who advocated for the poor. They established soup kitchens and taught classes for new immigrants and low-income homemakers. Social workers and nutrition experts also taught students practical skills regarding cooking safety, sanitation, nutrition and marketing.

Home economics was a progressive field that brought science to the home. It also brought women into higher education and leadership positions in public education, academia, government and industry.

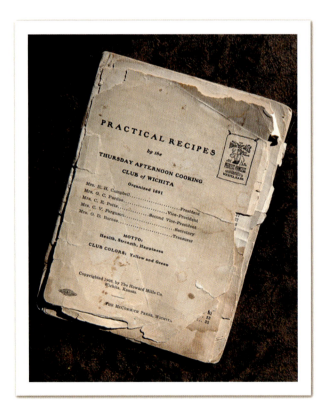

Practical Recipes, 1905

WICHITA CAKE

- 1 C SEEDED RAISINS OR CURRANTS
- ½ C BUTTER
- 1½ C SUGAR
- 1 C WATER OR MILK
- 1 TSP GROUND CLOVES
- 1 T GROUND CINNAMON
- 1 TSP NUTMEG, GRATED
- PINCH OF BLACK PEPPER
- 3 EGGS BEATEN SEPARATELY
- 2½ C PEERLESS PRINCESS FLOUR (ALL-PURPOSE)
- 2 ROUNDED TSP BAKING POWDER
- 2 TSP BAKING SODA

Preheat oven to 350°F. Generously grease a 12-inch Bundt pan or a 9x13 cake pan. In a medium sauce pan, combine raisins, sugar, water, butter and spices. Bring to a boil. Remove from heat and cool completely. Pour into a mixing bowl. In a medium bowl, whisk together flour, baking powder and baking soda.

Whisk eggs into cooled spice mixture until uniformly combined. Add the flour mixture in batches, whisking well after each addition. Pour batter into prepared pan and bake for 50-55 minutes or until toothpick inserted comes out clean. Cool completely.

Glaze In a small bowl whisk together ¾ cups powdered sugar, 2 tablespoons milk and ½ teaspoon vanilla. Drizzle over cooled cake.

A BRIDGE TO MODERNITY

At the turn of the 20th century, home economics was largely associated with coeducational land-grant institutions such as Kansas State University. From its inception, collegiate home economics was multidisciplinary, with an emphasis on science applied to the real world of the home, families and communities. Their work in fields such as fiber science, design and consumer economics made them central to the growth of the consumer economy. Throughout the first half of the 20th century, collegiate programs prepared thousands of women for public school teaching but also for careers in the extension service, state and federal governments, industry, hospitals, restaurants and hotels. Home economics served as a critical bridge for women from domesticity in the 19th century to modernity in the 20th century.

Professional home economics had two major goals: to teach women to assume their new roles as modern consumers, and to communicate homemakers' needs to manufacturers and political leaders.

THE ROLES OF WOMEN

Members were very interested in issues related to the roles of women – in households and careers. They wrote essays about the preferred role – housewife or career? The minutes asked "Could a woman have both a career and a happy household?" And they believed in the science of homemaking, studying the ideal kitchen layout. They tried to be more efficient household managers. And yet, they almost always listed themselves by their husband's names. As you see in this book, researching their history was accomplished through news reports about their husbands.

DETAILS FROM A YEARBOOK

A 1905 – 1906 yearbook included a detailed constitution and by-laws for the club. The by-laws set an allotment of $3.50 for hostesses to prepare each luncheon for the entire group. (That would be equivalent to $105 in 2018) There was an admission fee (membership) of one dollar, and every member was to pay dues of 15 cents per meeting whether present or absent.

The ladies were persevering in their quest to learn new cooking techniques. Each member was assigned to give a demonstration sometime during the year on one of the following: broiling, potato crust, pickled oysters, boning fish and fowl, tomato bisque, griddle cakes, steamed puddings, frozen desserts and leftovers.

1904 ST. LOUIS WORLD'S FAIR AND FOOD SAFETY

The 1904 World's Fair took place at an important historical turning point in American food culture. The way Americans ate was undergoing a radical transformation. For a few brief months, the fair captured an entire culture of eating that was being remade for the modern world.

During the early decades of the 20th century, the foods Americans ate depended primarily upon who they were (ethnic heritage, religious traditions), where they lived, and how much money they had to spend. Waves of immigrants introduced new foods and flavors, many opening restaurants. The first Italian-style pizzeria opened in New York City in 1905.

From pie-eating contests to funnel cake, food has always been a central part of fairs. This was especially true of the first World's Fairs, which provided hungry patrons with a thrilling introduction to "authentic" delicacies from exotic locales like China, Turkey and Morocco. The list of new treats attributed to the Fair is long, if somewhat inaccurate, and includes hot dogs, hamburgers, ice cream cones, banana splits, iced tea, Dr Pepper, cotton candy and peanut butter.

More importantly, food manufacturers were flooding our markets with new convenience foods, not all of which were healthy. A huge array of businesses sought ways to ensure and enlarge customer demand. They embraced merchandising, packaging and advertising with the goal of creating a national market of consumers, and to systematize desire.

THE PURE FOOD AND DRUG ACT

While the fair was in its closing weeks, a young writer named Upton Sinclair headed to Chicago to visit slaughterhouses, and published his investigations as *The Jungle* in 1906. It was a lurid critique of the meatpacking industry. The book exposed workplace conditions so filthy and exploitative that President Theodore Roosevelt felt compelled to act. His efforts and those of other reformers culminated in the Pure Food and Drug Act of 1906, the first major piece of legislation to outlaw adulterated or mislabeled food products, and was the beginning of federal oversight of the nation's food supply.

Alarmed by The Pure Food and Drug Act, normal people began to worry about the safety of their food. This worried food manufacturers, who grouped together and began to present "Pure Food Shows" that traveled all around the country and attracted huge audiences at fairs, shops and baseball fields. The point was to show that consumers had nothing to fear from their products.

The Wichita Eagle, **January 29, 1909**
The Thursday Afternoon Cooking Club was entertained at a luncheon at George Innes & Co. department store. The occasion was a "Pure Food Show." In addition to promoting food safety, the Shredded Wheat Biscuit Company demonstrated new uses for their prepared foods. The menu included:

OYSTER COCKTAIL WITH
TRISCUIT CROUTONS

CHICKEN FRICASSE ON
SHREDDED WHEAT
BISCUIT TOAST

MUSHROOMS IN
BISCUIT BASKETS

SARATOGA CHIPS
(POTATO CHIPS)

FRESH FRUIT SALAD

TRISCUITS WITH
ROYAL LUNCHEON CHEESE

CHILLED FRUITS WITH
ONE MINUTE GELATINE,
IN PATTIE SHELLS

STEFFENS
INDIVIDUAL CREAMS

ASSORTED CAKE

TRISCUIT CONFECTIONS

MINT COFFEE,
DISTILLED WATER

PERFECTION SALAD

½ C SUGAR
⅓ C RICE VINEGAR
2 T FRESH LEMON JUICE
2 T UNFLAVORED POWDERED GELATIN, SOFTENED IN ½ CUP COLD WATER
1 TSP KOSHER SALT
2 C CHOPPED CELERY
1 C FINELY SHREDDED CABBAGE
2 JARRED PIMENTOS, MINCED
1 GREEN BELL PEPPER, CORED, SEEDED, AND MINCED
COOKING SPRAY

Stir together sugar, vinegar, lemon juice, gelatin and salt in a small saucepan over medium heat to boiling; chill 30 minutes. Stir in remaining ingredients.

Spray a 12x4x2½-inch loaf pan, and transfer gelatin mixture to mold. Chill until set, about 6 hours. To release salad from mold, slide a knife along the edge of the mold; set mold in a bowl of hot water for 5 seconds. Invert salad onto a serving dish. Serve slices to accompany meat or other dishes.

Serves 12.

TACC member Chris Kubik remembers the Perfection Salad and other Jell-O salads her mother used to turn out for family gatherings. Her mother had a large collection of molds for that purpose.

Secretary's Minutes, October 27, 1910
A very pretty red and white luncheon was served by the hostesses. Red geraniums were used as table decorations. The menu was as follows. Cherry bullion with wafers, white fish with tomato sauce, escalloped potatoes with pimentos, creamed celery in red pepper shells, jelly sandwiches, Perfection Salad, Maraschino pudding and coffee.

PERFECTION SALAD

This is the first mention of Perfection Salad being prepared for the club. From the early years of the century, Perfection Salad was considered the epitome of edgy, healthy food. It later became a standby in school cafeterias where it seemed to meet all the requirements for scientific cooking – it contained fresh vegetables and fruit of many colors, so it was healthy, and it was beautiful. For years it went to potluck dinners everywhere.

JELL-O

Gelatin was once considered a sign of wealth. It is a protein produced from collagen (a gelatinous substance) extracted by boiling bones, which took hours to render. It was a messy, smelly and lengthy process that included straining and clarifying before it could be turned into aspic, fancy molded salads or spectacular frothy desserts. The use of gelatin was a sign that the host or hostess had the means to support a kitchen staff with the skill and time to create such a dish. Even after gelatin became available commercially it retained its air of culinary sophistication.

Francie Copeland

My grandmother was a member of TACC sometime in the mid-1900s. Her hands-down favorite dessert was lemon angel pie, which she learned to make at cooking club. I have used her recipe many times. It isn't easy getting the meringue just right, but TACC members are still making this 1915 recipe.

A POPULAR FOOD OVER THE YEARS

One favorite dish that has endured in the club is angel pie, a sort of upside down meringue pie. This pie was introduced to the club in the early years of the 20th century. It has appeared on menus many times including a recent spectacular lemon version for a Christmas luncheon. That pie was decorated with sprinkles and frosting snowdrops – a beautiful creation – and a very rich dessert.

ANGEL PIE
DECEMBER 23, 2015, BY VINTAGE RECIPES

4 EGGS, SEPARATED
1 TSP CREAM OF TARTAR
1½ C SUGAR, DIVIDED
1 LEMON, JUICE AND GRATED RIND
½ C HEAVY CREAM, WHIPPED
FRUIT FOR GARNISHMENT

Preheat oven to 350°F.

Beat eggs whites until very stiff. Add cream of tartar when just fluffy. Slowly add 1 cup of the sugar and beat (says for 15 minutes but this is assuming hand mixing.)

Place mixture in buttered pie tin. Bake 1 hour. Cool. In double boiler beat egg yolk with ½ cup sugar. Add lemon juice and grated rind. Stir and cook until thickened. Cool filling and pour over baked meringue. Top with whipped cream. Garnish with strawberries or other fruit if desired.

TECHNOLOGY IN THE NEW CENTURY

After 1900, gas companies turned to the kitchen as the source of a new market. Since gas ranges had no need for the heavy, cast iron box of a wood or coal-burning range, they could be built in much lighter and more compact forms. Plus, gas ranges gave off much less excess heat and had no need for a chimney, making them ideal for the new, smaller kitchens. What's more, they were light enough to stand on tall, slender legs to become, along with sinks, one of several pieces of freestanding furniture in the early modern kitchen.

MENU SELECTIONS

Food choices in these years were becoming more sophisticated and new cooking techniques were being explored. Some of the menus were quite imaginative. Unfortunately, we have no recipes for the eleven-dish lunch including roast whole pig from February 1914.

Very soon the beginning of World War I interrupted the planning for the cookbook. It was eventually published in 1922 as *Wichita Cooking Club Cook Book*.

THE CLUB'S TWENTY-FIFTH ANNIVERSARY

Oscar and Ida Barnes House, the site of the 25th Anniversary meal, is located in Wichita's Midtown neighborhood and was completed in 1911. It is an excellent example of the Italian Renaissance style and is listed on the Register of Historic Places. Oscar Barnes was a pioneer druggist and music dealer. He built the Michigan Building, just 25 feet wide and six stories tall, which was known as Wichita's "skinniest skyscraper" until it was demolished in 2015.

Barnes Home, 901 N. Broadway

Secretary's Minutes, February 5, 1914 The decorations were beautiful potted ferns. A roast young pig with a red apple in its mouth and parsley decoration was carved and served by the hostess. The menu was roast young pig with dressing and gravy, baked apples, Kansas sweet potatoes, corn bread, head lettuce with Roquefort cheese dressing, watermelon pickles, apricot whip.

Secretary's Minutes, April 13, 1916 (Publishing) a cookbook was again discussed and an individual opinion by every member followed – which finally resulted in a decision to go ahead with the book and get it out as a Christmas edition. If every member bought ten dollars' worth of books, it would cover the cost of a first edition of 500 copies. Each member would be responsible for 20 recipes.

Secretary's Minutes, December 14, 1916 An old fashioned dinner was served buffet style. Hostesses defeated the high cost of living by preparing the meal at a cost of 11 cents per person. Menu: Rice with cheese, sweet potato apples, country sausage (donated), buttermilk biscuit, custard pie, coffee, amber marmalade, olives.

25th Anniversary Luncheon
Secretary's Minutes, December 28, 1916 Mrs. O.D. Barnes (Ida) hosted a delicious luncheon for twenty of the Club's current members and eleven ex-members. All marched in twos into the dining room to be served a buffet-style luncheon in two courses, of fresh salmon in shells with tartar sauce, relishes, boned turkey, ribbon potatoes, brown and white bread sandwiches, cranberry jelly, fruit salad, fig pudding and divinity candy. At roll call, each member responded with reminiscences, and told what year they came into the Club. Mrs. Barnes read a list of all people who had been members. Each member brought a tested recipe for the new cookbook.

Secretary's Minutes, February 22, 1917 Washington's Birthday luncheon at the home of Mrs. Chester I. Long (Anna). The tables were most attractive with a centerpiece of flags, cherries and hatchets in profusion. George Washington postcards were inscribed with the following menu: Colonial Cup, Martha Washington Chicken Pie, Nellie Custer salad, Hatchet Gems, Revolutionary pickles, Strawberry Preserves, White House Coffee, Washington Cake. The meeting was held in Senator Long's spacious library before a charming open fire. During the luncheon, the ladies were entertained by strains from an Edison concealed in the breakfast room.

4

WORLD WAR COMES TO AMERICA

On April 6, 1917, the United States entered into World War I. More than 2 million U.S. soldiers eventually fought on battlefields in France.

The war was unprecedented in its brutality. Servicemen and women came home with injuries to their bodies and minds. TACC members visited hospitals bringing cookies, blankets and sweaters. They wrote letters for veterans who had mobility problems and were sincere in their efforts to help the disabled.

FOOD WILL WIN THE WAR

Shortly after the United States entered the war, the U.S. Food Administration was established to manage the wartime supply of food. Appointed head of the administration by President Woodrow Wilson, future President Herbert Hoover developed a voluntary program that relied on Americans' compassion and sense of patriotism to support the larger war effort. Posters urging citizens to reduce their personal consumption of meat, wheat, fats and sugar were plastered throughout communities. Slogans such as "Food will win the war" compelled people to avoid wasting precious groceries and encouraged them to eat a multitude of fresh fruits and vegetables, which were too difficult to transport overseas. Likewise, promotions such as "Meatless Tuesdays" and "Wheatless Wednesdays" implored Americans to voluntarily modify their eating habits in order to increase shipments to the valiant soldiers defending our freedom.

SUPPORT FOR THE RED CROSS

The war affected the club in many ways. They discussed food and the domestic economy and formed a committee to report on such subjects as home canning, drying of fruits and vegetables, war bread and other topics. The club agreed to cut menus to simpler and less expensive foods, and to give the money saved to the Red Cross. They continued to collect dues during the summer even though they were not meeting, and added the money to the Red Cross Fund.

WAR BREAD AND FLOUR

A Wheat Commission was formed to ensure adequate supplies of bread, so that it did not need to be rationed. War bread came to contain additions of barley, oats or rye flour, and later, with added soybean or potato flour. The bread was consequently dark in color. People were also encouraged to make their own bread by mixing the flour with precooked rice or potatoes, as well as haricot beans or barley, to make the flour go further.

COOKBOOK FOR PRESSURE STEAM COOKER

The pressure cooker was an amazing device for cooks in the early days of the century. It was used on any kind of stove, and achieved much shorter cooking times for meats and vegetables. It was frequently used for canning. To keep soot from sticking to the bottom, the user was advised to coat it with clean grease.

The "cheaper" cuts of meat are most nutritious, according to the cookbook, and are made more delicious by quicker pressure cooking. The book addresses the process for sealing tin cans with solder before pressure cooking. It even advertises a new invention The Burpee Can Sealer for tin cans, "giving a new impetus to home canning." The back cover announces "Hygienic Living is the Foundation of Morality."

WORK RESUMES ON NEW COOKBOOK

After the war ended in late 1918, the club felt free to resume work on the cookbook they had begun planning back in 1913. Once again, every member was required to submit tested recipes as well as household hints.

Secretary's Minutes, November 8, 1917 Meatless, sugarless, wheatless luncheon. Menu: Escalloped oysters with macaroni, bean salad from the garden, cherry preserves, beaten biscuits, pumpkin pie flavored with honey, coffee. After the luncheon various plans were considered by which the Club could help win the war or help the soldiers. It was agreed to stick to simple menus of three articles, and as soon as possible eliminate wheat and meat and substitute other forms and fish food. Each member pledged to make one sweater for a Kansas soldier and report at the next meeting how little sugar her family had used in the interval of two weeks.

Secretary's Minutes, February 14, 1918 The menu was creamed sweetbreads with potato crust, grapefruit salad, bran gems, grape preserves, chocolate snow with cookies. The afternoon was given to a demonstration of the uses of war flour (in making) delicious puff pastry and a war cake made previously.

Secretary's Minutes, May 1918 Red snapper with tartar sauce in ramekins, vegetable salad, toast and cheese sandwiches, preserved peaches, bread pudding with maple sugar hard sauce. It was suggested and approved that the Cooking Club give a dinner at $1.00 per plate to earn money for yarn to be used in the two knitting machines available for Club use.

Secretary's Minutes, February 13, 1919 Only 13 members were present to enjoy and profit by a member's demonstration of her pressure steam cooker. Roast of beef, carrots, and potatoes were steamed for the luncheon. There were delicious biscuits, gravy and the pineapple soufflé, a very pretty change from the usual white pineapple gelatin puddings.

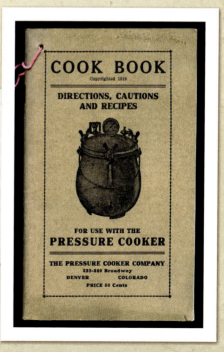

Secretary's Minutes, April 25, 1920 Luncheon menu chicken salad, new potatoes in parsley butter, asparagus on toast and strawberry shortcake. The subject of stoves was discussed. The inadequate gas supply has made it necessary to test out other means of cooking, and the electric stoves received excellent reports as substitutes for the gas and coal stoves.

Note: The U.S. economy expanded wildly as a result of its participation in the war. People were buying cars and other new appliances and conveniences. The public saw a shortage of oil and gas supplies, but according to Standard Oil, "It is not a case of diminished supply, but one of increased consumption." The price of gasoline increased more than 60% in one year.

Secretary's Minutes, January 21, 1921
Mrs. Campbell reported a committee has visited the sick soldiers and given them fruit and magazines. Mrs. Brown reported that her committee had taken a bath robe and slippers to a child in the tuberculosis camp, and brought a thank you note from the child.

Secretary's Minutes, March 30, 1922 A Cuban luncheon was served of oranges served Cuban style, yellow rice with chicken in casserole with vegetables. Waffles were served as the dessert with maple syrup and were given as a demonstration of cooking on the electric waffle iron.

ELECTRIC STOVES SLOW TO CATCH ON

The electric stove was showcased at the Chicago World's Fair in 1893. Unlike the gas stove, the electric stove was slow to catch on, partly due to the need for cities and towns to be electrified. By the 1930s, the technology had matured and the electric stove slowly began to replace the gas stove, especially in household kitchens.

BETWEEN THE WARS

A SELF-SERVICE GROCERY STORE

1916 was a big year for food shoppers. The first supermarket, a Piggly Wiggly store, opened in Memphis and rapidly spread across the southern part of the nation. Wichita had its first Piggly Wiggly in the early 1920s.

A culture-changing phenomenon, this was the first true self-service grocery store, and the originator of other now-familiar supermarket features such as checkout stands, individual-item price marking and especially shopping carts. You could peruse shelves loaded with items you saw being advertised. People loved these clean and sparkling stores just as they loved the enticing soup cans and chocolate bars they could pluck off the shelves and drop in their baskets. Supermarket labeling was the birthplace of branding.

In 1913, J. S. Dillon and Sons Store had opened in Hutchinson, Kansas. It was the first cash-and-carry grocery in the state. Ray Dillon began attending marketing meetings and gradually adapted the new self-service features first incorporated by Piggly Wiggly. Dillons, now part of Kroger, are the predominant supermarkets in Kansas.

THE CLUB WILL PUBLISH A COOKBOOK – FINALLY

The club began collecting recipes and household hints for the desired new cookbook in 1913. Members were required to bring tested recipes written out on cards and handed to the secretary. As previously noted, the club had decided to publish in 1916 but found it needed to delay. After the war, the cookbook again became a priority. A great many of the recipes published were submitted by Ellen Campbell.

Introduction from
The Thursday Afternoon Cooking Club's Cook Book, 1922

Great credit for the success of the Club, in organizing and planning all work, should be given to Mrs. B.H. Campbell, who gave the best of her time, strength, and advice as President for eleven years. The love and harmony that has always been with the Club we owe to her firm, yet gentle advice; so much so, that we feel she was the Mother of the Club. We are now in our thirty-first year, and the only one of the Charter members left to enjoy the club is Mrs. O.D. Barnes.

For many years, the one great desire of the Club has been to have a cookbook, containing our very choicest receipts, not for financial profit, but to be a guide and help to the generations that follow the earnest women who have striven for so many years to bring wholesome living into the homes.

We could not publish the book without acknowledging the deep obligation we owe to our dear departed member, Mrs. Chester I. Long, whose kindness, faithful work, and generous co-operation has made the book possible. This feeling of appreciation will find glad echo in the hearts of all the members, and of all others who receive the book.

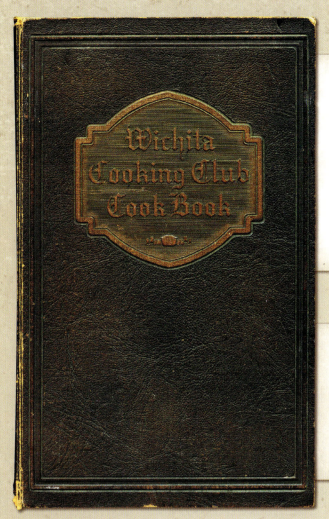

Secretary's Minutes, October 21, 1921 A called meeting was held to discuss the cookbook. It was decided that the book will be published and the club will personally finance it. A committee was appointed to attend a demonstration at the Forum on canning vegetables. (From 1912 to 1965, the Forum on South Water Street served as the city's arena, main auditorium, convention center and exposition hall.)

Secretary's Minutes, December 9, 1922
The committee served a meatless luncheon. Mrs. Campbell, a committee of one, reported that the cookbook will be out by the 15th of November. She urged members to get busy and dispose of them.

Secretary's Minutes, November 8, 1923
Buffet luncheon consisting of creamed oysters with spaghetti in ramekins, squash soufflé, fruit salad, chocolate charlotte. Mrs. Campbell reported on cookbook money and price of publication of 500 more books. When all books are sold there will be approximately $245 in the treasury. Five hundred more books would cost $850.00. The majority were not in favor of publishing more books.

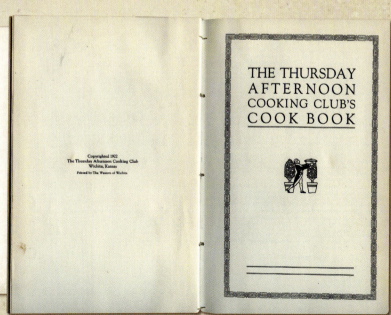

THINGS YOU SHOULD KNOW
FROM THE COOKBOOK

To Make Washing Fluid

1 can of lye
2 oz of salts of tartar
2 ½ gallons of water
2 oz of lump ammonia
1 lb of borax in lump

Use one cup in a boiler of water, with soap cut fine.

To Pack Eggs

Put 1 quart liquid glass (liquid sodium silicate also called Isinglass) in stone jar with 12 quarts water. Add fresh eggs as you get them. Note: This method is still in use today.

Making Out a Menu

Making out a menu for breakfasts and dinners every day for a week saves much wear and tear on the home maker's thought machine. Lunch can be a time to use leftovers. Every good housewife knows the importance of having novelty in the meals.

Oven Temperatures

(Ovens in those days did not have thermometers.)

A slow oven In five minutes glazed paper will brown.

A medium oven In three minutes glazed paper will brown.

A hot oven In two minutes glazed paper will brown.

Making A Frying Compound

Suet at the present time is 10c./lb. Lard is 28c. From 1 lb. (suet) can be obtained 14 oz. fat. To this can be added 1 part of oil to 2 parts of suet. Cottonseed oil or corn oil can be used. Suet has harder consistency and the oil reduces it to the consistency of lard. 1 part beef suet and 2 parts leaf lard – pork – makes a fine frying mixture.

Lawn Suggestions

Grass seed will germinate in from 14 to 18 days

RECIPES FROM THE 1922 TACC COOKBOOK

POTATO SPLIT BISCUIT   PAGE 12

- 1 CAKE COMPRESSED YEAST
- 1 TSP SALT
- 2 EGGS
- 1 T SUGAR
- 2 LARGE POTATOES
- 3 PTS FLOUR
- 1 C LARD AND BUTTER MIXED
- 1 C SWEET MILK

About 6:30 o'clock put yeast to soak in the milk. Bake the potatoes so they will be well done by 9:00. Put through a ricer or sieve. Into the hot potato put lard and butter previously creamed. Add salt and sugar and eggs well beaten. Add yeast and milk to 2 pts. of the flour. Let stand. Two hours before dinner place on molding board. Roll about ½ inch thick. Cut with large cutter. Spread one biscuit with soft butter and place another biscuit on top. Stick thru with finger. Let rise and bake in moderate oven ½ hour. Butter, sugar and cinnamon can be added over top of these biscuits with pleasing effect.

STRAWBERRY MOUSSE   PAGE 205

- 2 C WHIPPING CREAM
- 1 C POWDERED SUGAR
- 2 C MASHED STRAWBERRIES

Whip cream stiff, add sugar and berries, turn into a mold and cover with oiled paper – cover tight. Pack in 4 parts ice and 1 part salt. Let stand 3 hours.

GOOD FRIDAY EGGS   PAGE 296

- 6 SLICES BREAD
- 1½ C MILK
- 6 EGGS
- ¼ TSP SALT
- 6 T BUTTER
- 6 T CHEESE

Cut bread into thick slices and fry each slice in 1 tablespoon butter. Beat eggs, add milk and salt. Pour over fried bread in large shallow pan, and bake 15 minutes. Grate cheese and sprinkle over mixture when taken from oven.

RECIPES FROM THE 1922 TACC COOKBOOK

BRAMBLES PAGE 253

1 C RAISINS
1 C SUGAR
CHERRY PRESERVES

CRUST
2 C FLOUR
1 C BUTTER
6 T ICE WATER

Revised in 2018.

Preheat oven to 375°F. Mix the flour and butter, moisten with the ice water and roll out as for pie crust. Roll out the crust ⅛-inch thick. Cut into 4½-inch circles. Spread one half of each circle with the preserves. Fold the other half over it, pinch the edges together. Place on non-stick cookie sheet or Silpat liner and bake 20 to 25 minutes. This will make little cakes like hand pies when done. Very good for luncheon. By Mrs. B.H. Campbell.

A NEW ERA OF ORGANIZATION

Following the publication of the cookbook, the members found a need to organize their recipe-keeping. Some committees were organized, but didn't provide the kind of filing system they wanted. Interestingly the seven appointed committees did not include main dishes.

PICNIC AT CLEAR LAKE

Clear Lake was a pleasure resort near Garden Plain, stocked for fishing. TACC spent many spring and summer meetings at Mrs. C.L. Davidson's luxurious home there. "Watch Wichita Win" was a motto originated by C.L. Davidson in 1909 when he was mayor. A large electric banner illuminated the motto over the street.

ANNUAL DINNER WITH HUSBANDS

In 1915 Henry J. Allen and his wife, Elsie, hired architect Frank Lloyd Wright to design a house for them in Wichita. The Allens lived in the Prairie-style house until 1947. It is one of few structures in Kansas with designs by Wright. Mr. Allen was the 21st Governor of Kansas and was appointed U.S. Senator from Kansas in 1929. The Allens hosted the annual dinner in 1926.

COOKING DEMONSTRATION

Super Maid was a line of aluminum cookware advertised as being solid, seamless and just like silver in appearance. Because the lids sealed tightly to prevent loss of moisture from the food, it was promoted as being "waterless." A lower cooking temperature was also recommended, although that may have had more to do with aluminum's propensity to warp under high heat. Due to its excellent heat conductivity aluminum cookware was made with wooden handles.

TACC WINS A BLUE RIBBON

Walter P. Innes, a native Kansan, bought a small Wichita mercantile in 1896. In 1907 he designed and built a huge new store, placing it at the corner of Broadway and William. His uncle George Innes helped finance the store, and thus was honored by the store's new name. As the first big downtown merchant he helped other businesses into the area. By the 1920s Innes had become a tastemaker, hence the name for the Innes table-setting contest. The Innes Tea Room was a popular and fashionable dining room well into the 1960s.

OCTOBER 29, 1929, THE CRASH OF WALL STREET

The 1930s were the years of the Great Depression. After the stock market crash, Americans were changing the way they cooked and ate.

By 1932 nearly thirty million Americans had lost their source of income, from unemployment or loss of a family breadwinner. Rural people were heading to the cities and learning to cook on hotplates in rented rooms because they did not have money for diners.

Frank Lloyd Wright-designed Allen House

During the Depression, self-sufficiency carried over into social life. One-dish suppers and church potlucks were important ways to have fun and share food. On radio and in women's magazines, home economists taught women how to stretch their food budgets with casseroles and meals like creamed chipped beef on toast or waffles. Chili, macaroni and cheese, soups and creamed chicken were popular meals. Many people who lived through that period have fond memories of the tastes and smells of that era, including candy-coated carrots, mock apple pie, mock whipped cream and tea instead of coffee.

Today we recognize many items used in the home during the 1930s as collectibles, including Depression Glass. The dime store, where the thrifty homemaker could find everything from toiletries to household goods, was a common source for this inexpensive purchase. At a time when a loaf of bread cost about a nickel, frugal shoppers could also buy a piece of Depression glass for around the same price. Even the pattern names – American Sweetheart, Royal Princess – alluded to better times and a longing for the glamorous lifestyles of the 1920s.

Secretary's Minutes, May 14, 1925
What is so rare as a May day fair, when we went to Clear Lake, there to partake of the food you can't beat which is always a treat. Mrs. Warren Brown drove out in her new Packard car which went so fast she drove miles too far.

Secretary's Minutes, January 7, 1926
The annual dinner given by the club to their husbands was held at the beautiful home of Mr. and Mrs. Henry J. Allen. After dinner the guests spent a very delightful evening playing bridge and other card games.

Secretary's Minutes, April 15, 1926
Mr. Price, who demonstrated the Super Maid Cookware where it is possible to cook without water, bake without an oven and fry without smoke, prepared the luncheon. The luncheon consisted of potatoes cooked skin-on without water, a roast, sweet potatoes and carrots cooked in a Dutch oven in a very short time with no water, and cake cooked on the top of the stove.

Secretary's Minutes, December 6, 1923
Our president caused quite a stir when she appointed seven chairmen of committees. The committees are as follows: Bread, Cake, Desserts, Jellies, Pies, Quick remedies, Salad. Mrs. Davidson asked us each to be ready with ten correct recipes on each subject for our first meeting in January.

Secretary's Minutes, January 17, 1924
It was finally decided that the chairman of each committee would purchase uniform books in which to hold recipes. Each chairman to be responsible for recipes on her subject. Note: These new recipe books have not survived in the collection of the club. There is little mention in future minutes of the activities of these committees except for a revision in 1929.

Secretary's Minutes, January 3, 1924
A committee was formed to consider purchasing uniform books for recipes for all club members.

THE LAST YEARS OF THE ICE BOX?

In the early 1900s, many American households stored the perishable food in an insulated "ice box" that was usually made of wood and lined with tin or zinc. A large block of ice was stored inside to keep the food chilled.

By 1930, many Americans happily began giving up their ice boxes filled with melting ice for a newly affordable electric refrigerator. It was unthinkable to throw away food during the Great Depression, and refrigerator sales grew rapidly thanks to manufacturer's discounted prices.

The real bump in refrigerators, however, started in 1935, when New Deal loans encouraged Americans to switch to electric.

Did they use an ice box or a fridge? Interestingly, TACC meetings during the 1930s through 1940s reflect frequent offerings of ice box pudding, ice box cake, ice box rolls, ice box angel food cake, almond ice box cake and lemon ice box cake. We know that 10% of households owned a refrigerator in 1930, so probably most TACC members would have been using a refrigerator to make these "ice box" foods.

General Electric produced cookbooks that gave tips on transforming Sunday's roast into something new and delicious for later in the week. Looking for new ways to store leftover food, Tupperware became commonplace. The distinctive "burp" meant that the container was sealed, promising longer lives for leftovers.

A DYNASTY OF HOSTESSES

In 1937, its 46th year, *The Wichita Beacon* society editor, Ruth Vawter Rankin, called TACC the "Southwest's Most Unique Club which includes on its roster the famous and gracious hostesses of yesteryear and hostesses of the present day, whose hospitality is coveted among the gourmets to whom dining is an art." She also called members the "arbiters of elegance, who instructed their daughters in the intricacies and lore of traditional recipes, many of which have been handed down as treasured recipes from the old countries. Many of the recipes have been modernized from the originals which were prepared in the eras of big families and fireplace cookery – involving spits, cauldrons, bain-maries."

According to Mrs. Rankin, the anniversary menu included Mrs. H.W. Lewis' famous Prune Pudding and Mrs. G.K. Purvis' date bread. Steamed fig pudding by Mrs. C.V. Ferguson is a favorite of the club; it was served with lemon sauce. Creole salmon potpourri used canned salmon served in a wreath of rice. Mrs. Finlay Ross shared her recipe for old fashioned ribbon cake, baked in two batters and put together with jelly.

ORIGINAL MINCE PIE RECIPE

"Pie of mutton or beef must be finely minced and seasoned with pepper and salt, and a little saffron to color it. Use suet or marrow in a good quantity, a little vinegar, prunes, grated raisins and dates. If you will have palest royal pastry, take butter and yolks of eggs and so temper the flour to make the paste," Gervase Markham, *The English Huswife, Containing the Inward and Outward Virtues Which Ought to Be in a Complete Woman*, 1615.

WORLD WAR II

On September 1, 1939, World War II began with the invasion of Poland by Nazi Germany and the subsequent declarations of war on Germany by France and the United Kingdom.

Club activities continued mostly unchanged during the early years of the war in Europe. They were not unaware of the action, but carried on with their meetings and luncheons.

The Plains states, especially Kansas and Nebraska, were actively isolationist. Kansas Senator Arthur Clapper was a fiery leader in the congressional effort to keep the country out of war. Because Clapper was elected five times and served 35 years in the Senate, it can be assumed that he represented the predominant views of Kansans and by extension, the ladies of the club.

President Roosevelt began using the Lend-Lease Act to supply Great Britain with what he called "surplus" military equipment – an expression of his view that we needed to help defend against German aggression. This activity was fiercely protested by Senator Clapper.

The predominant isolationist was Charles Lindbergh, the famous pilot who gained much public sympathy because of the kidnapping and killing of his baby. Lindbergh was a close personal friend of Hermann Goering and a naïve admirer of the great German war machine. And yet, following "Kristallnacht" or "Night of Broken Glass," the real beginning of pogroms against Jews, Lindbergh abandoned his German home and returned to the United States, still insisting the war was not our business.

GOLD-COVERED SOUVENIR BOOKLET FOR THE 50TH ANNIVERSARY

The booklet was a gift from the Garst Family Laundry business. It contained an unusually complex concoction called Bee Hive Soufflés, which were – believe it or not – served at a TACC luncheon. Individual strands of spaghetti were cooked, cooled and then wound one at a time around the inside of a small mold. The mold was filled with cheese soufflé mixture and baked. When finished, the molds were turned out so that the spaghetti hive held the upside-down soufflé.

WWII BRINGS SERIOUS RATIONING

Club members had no way of knowing that just three days after their 50th Anniversary Celebration our country would be attacked by the Japanese, or that the United States would very soon declare war, but they were most certainly aware of the climate of war in the U.S.

Minutes from the war years tell of the efforts members made to do their part, and the difficulties they endured when wartime shortages required rationing.

Food was in short supply because much of the processed and canned foods were reserved for shipping overseas to our military and our Allies; transportation of fresh foods was limited due to gasoline and tire rationing. Imported foods, like coffee and sugar, were limited due to restrictions on importing.

Secretary's Minutes, October 11, 1928
Menu: Dutch meat rolls, parsley potatoes, grape conserve, jellied tomato salad and wafers, sliced dill pickles, celery, peach cobbler with whipped cream, coffee and mints. Twenty-five members and two guests were seated at two long tables with beautiful appointments. Homer Harden arrived and took pictures of the members and guests on the garden steps.

Secretary's Minutes, January 3, 1929
Hostesses served a lovely luncheon of tomato puree, cheese wafers, Old Virginia spiced ham with raisin sauce, escalloped potatoes, red cinnamon apple salad, orange biscuits, currant jelly, curried pickles, steamed fruit pudding, caramel sauce and hard sauce with rum. Discussion resulted about the first place prize the Club won in the Innes table-setting contest. The blue ribbon will be placed in the minute book and the prize of $25 will be sent to the Tuberculous Home as our yearly good-will greeting, along with two rocking chairs donated by members.

Secretary's Minutes, December 3, 1931
The committee served a most delicious and unusual as well as economical luncheon of fruit cocktail with wheat wafers, Italian soup with noodles and grated cheese, home-baked bread, pickles and celery and graham cracker pie.

Secretary's Minutes, December 18, 1930
Mrs. Norton reported on cases she had found of old people that were in need of help. Motion carried to allow $50 to be used as she saw fit. Another motion allocated $23.24 to pay a bill at Steele Hardware Co. for necessities for the family.

Secretary's Minutes, October 13, 1932
There was a decision made to donate monies which were unused by hostess committees to the Home for the Aged.

Secretary's Minutes, December 15, 1932
Boned duck Chinese style, with water chestnut dressing, baked onions in cream, apple sauce in timbales, rice and green olives, apricot upside down cake with whipped cream. Since there are so many needy people, a decision was made to spend $265 from the reserve fund (cookbook fund) for the Salvation Army Soup Kitchen and other charities.

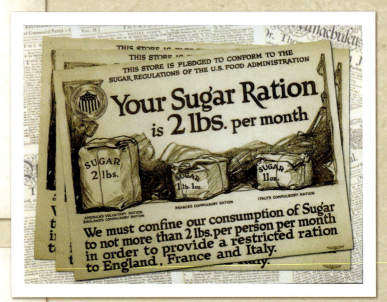

Secretary's Minutes, December 17, 1932
The committee asked for a food basket to be given to a needy family. $50 was allocated for other baskets and necessities to be given to needy families. The beautiful decorations included a huge snow ball on the large table. The snow ball contained individually wrapped gifts for the members which were Mrs. Gilkeson's delicious homemade caramels.

Secretary's Minutes, October 12, 1933
The forty-second anniversary was celebrated at the home of Mrs. Horn. The menu committee served an old-fashioned luncheon, one that might have been served forty years ago. Chicken croquettes with mushrooms, cranberry sauce, potato salad, carrots in pastry cups, sliced oranges with tartar sauce, hot biscuits, floating island, and a four-tiered birthday cake baked and decorated by Mrs. Gilkeson. Dues were set at $7.50 a year. The members paid tribute to Mrs. Spangler, their founder and first president, who died recently. Her untiring efforts in times of duress were noted. She was a zealous worker, inspiring all by her high ideals.

Secretary's Minutes, April 26, 1934
Two long unusually attractive tables were set with lace cloths, blue stemmed glassware, and tiny blue glass May baskets filled with flowers. The menu included boned stuffed duck, buttered new peas, tomato cups with fresh asparagus tips, hot rolls, quince jelly, relishes, baked Mary Anns filled with French ice cream and fresh strawberries, crepe suzette, and glazed Brazil nuts. Mrs. Norton demonstrated making crepes suzettes and Mrs. Rex showed how to de-bone a duck. Mrs. Buck gave everyone dainty jars of preserves.

RATIONING

Every American was issued a series of ration books. These contained removable stamps good for certain rationed items like sugar, meat, cooking oil and canned goods. A person could not buy a rationed item without giving the grocer the right ration stamp. For a club based on food and cooking, this was serious business.

THE WAR ENDS

May 9, 1945. Germany surrendered, ending the war in Europe. On August 15, Emperor Hirohito announced Japan's surrender.

MISSING MINUTES

There is a fifteen-year-gap in TACC minute books between 1948 and 1963, but TACC persevered during the decades after World War II. The scrapbooks contain clippings from newspaper stories and a full-page story about the TACC 60th Anniversary. In the absence of minutes, we rely on Mrs. Rankin's descriptions in the newspaper.

SIXTY-TWO YEARS OLD

The Wichita Beacon, **February 29, 1953** When the cooking club marked its sixty-second anniversary on February 29, 1953, the setting, as described by Ruth Vawter Rankin, society editor for *The Wichita Beacon*, was a resplendent display of yellow and wine colored mums centering the large tables. Wine and yellow were also reflected in the colors of the menu. There was a cranberry gelatin salad, veal croquettes with a mushroom sauce, frosted sweet potatoes, individual mince pies, relish plate and Mrs. Jameyson's famous Oregon grape jelly. "Still," said Mrs. Rankin, "the members are quick to try out new cake and roll mixes, and take advantage of every new cooking phase in an attempt to keep on their cooking toes."

The Wichita Eagle, **March 23, 1957** Members gather around to try out the menu for the day at a regular meeting of the 66-year-old club. The meal featured veal birds with bread stuffing and mushroom gravy, cinnamon apples, spiced peaches, pineapple-cucumber salad, plum pudding with hard sauce.

The Wichita Eagle, **November 5, 1959** "Quality Cooking An Art – Modern table settings are lovely, but not more beautiful than the old-fashioned dinner arrangements of our mothers or grandmothers. … This fact was proven recently by members of the Thursday Afternoon Cooking Club when they celebrated the longevity of the organization at an 'old-fashioned' luncheon gathering. Mrs. Fred Little was hostess for the event at her Hillcrest apartment. The menu consisted of foods prepared from 'practical recipes that have met the requirements of every-day experience and have pleased palates for many years.' Mrs. Paul Ross, club president, was in charge of preparation of the main dish."

"Mrs. Fred Little served from an elaborate gold-lined sterling coffee service which is among the many pieces that belonged to her mother, Mrs. Finlay Ross, one of the first members. That service and other silver and crystal table appointments are more than 75 years old. An unusual silver butter mold held home-churned butter. Coin silver flatware that belonged to Mrs. Little's great-grandmother in Scotland, and Havilland china that is 100 years old were used on the dining tables. The meal was served in the style of the 19th century with silver spoon-holders and handsome casters for holding cruets and condiments enhancing the tables."

50th Anniversary Luncheon

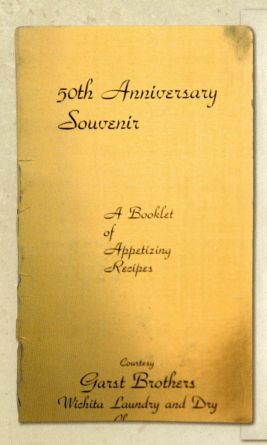

50th Anniversary Luncheon
Secretary's Minutes, December 4, 1941
Hosted by Mrs. Lewis, a member since the first year of the organization and an active member for 49 years. After the guests arrived, hot mulled cider was served in the living room. The members were asked to find their places marked by gold place cards. The centerpiece was a large birthday cake decorated with gold trimmings and gold leaves arranged around it. The service plates with gold mats and beautiful corsages of yellow mums added much to the gold color scheme and surely made a beautiful table. The Club colors, yellow and green, were carried out in the dessert. The menu committee served creamed chicken in puff pastry party shells, aspic salad with dressing, lovely relish tray, hot rolls and jelly, French vanilla ice cream with minted pineapple dressing, anniversary gold cake, coffee. The program was a reminiscence and story by members about the years past and clippings concerning the meetings. Letters from absent members were read. During the afternoon, pictures were taken of the Club.

Secretary's Minutes, November 20, 1941
The minutes as read will be revised by order of the committee. No further explanation was given for this extraordinary action.

Secretary's Minutes, April 21, 1938
The lovely luncheon consisted of fried chicken with cream gravy, hot biscuits, a lovely vegetable salad composed of fresh tomatoes, asparagus, cucumber, radishes and cottage cheese. Relishes, jelly and lemon sponge cake with whipped cream coconut and marshmallows.

Secretary's Minutes, February 6, 1941
The luncheon consisted of the following: old fashioned vegetable soup in small bowls served on plates with avocado, lime and orange salad in lettuce cups with salad dressing, Sally Lund bread, relish plate, banana mousse and southern ginger bread, coffee. After lunch, Mrs. Allen gave a short talk about British Relief efforts.

Secretary's Minutes, January 12, 1939
Mrs. Rex presented a mince pie made from the original recipe from 1394, on a silver platter, with his head on one end and long feathers set cunningly about him. Also, pineapple and pear salad with fruited mayonnaise, marshmallow pudding with whipped cream, chocolate cookies and candied orange peel.

Secretary's Minutes, May 8, 1942
Members are resigning to do war work. Meetings will be discontinued until the first of the year. Because of war rationing and cancellations, the hostesses will decide on serving choices and amounts.

Secretary's Minutes, January 14, 1943
The officers met previously to discuss new rationing by the government. Butter was at a premium, gasoline, meat, and all things that blue stamps buy, as well as red stamps, so one wonders how a luncheon can be prepared. The club will meet only once a month, on the second Thursday, while the war emergency lasts. Dues were cut to $4 for 8 months of meetings.

4 — UNITED STATES OF AMERICA — OFFICE OF PRICE ADMINISTRATION
WAR RATION BOOK FOUR
779123 FL

Issued to _____
(Print first, middle, and last names)

Complete address _____

READ BEFORE SIGNING
In accepting this book, I recognize that it remains the property of the United States Government. I will use it only in the manner and for the purposes authorized by the Office of Price Administration.

Void if Altered _____
(Signature)
It is a criminal offense to violate rationing regulations.
OPA Form R-145   16—35570-1

Secretary's Minutes, May 7, 1942
The club spent the afternoon sewing for war children.

Secretary's Minutes, October 9, 1941
The club decided we will celebrate our 50th anniversary.

BETTY CROCKER'S AMERICA

In the 1950s, 99 out of 100 homemakers knew Betty Crocker's name. Her *Picture Cook Book*, published in 1950, with a first printing of 950,000 copies, established her as a personality who presided over correspondence, advertising, radio and newspaper columns. Women searched for the chance to connect with someone who could solve their baking problems, even though, as we now know, Betty Crocker was a fictional person created to sell Gold Medal flour.

Some older members remember the foods their mothers served after the war. They recall oleo coming in plastic bags with a drop of coloring that could be worked into the white substance before use to make it look like butter. Of course, everyone remembers mac and cheese and PB&J sandwiches, plus cake mixes, roll mixes and precooked meats like bologna.

A decade after the war ended, the food industry faced the daunting challenge of trying to create a peacetime market for wartime foods. A great deal of technology was in place. Safe commercial canning processes, refrigeration, gas and electric stoves and refrigerated rail cars created a generational shift in thinking about the world of food.

There had been immense changes in food production. Farmers had begun to select crops with long-distance shipping in mind, not flavor, and chemicals were coming into use in raising livestock and poultry. Packaged foods were advertised everywhere, and recipes tied to their use were prominent in magazines and newspapers. The food industry supplied ads and greatly influenced editorial matter, encouraging the use of prepared foods.

FROZEN FOOD

Fresh from almost heroic production for the troops, frozen-food manufacturers declared that fresh produce for retail consumption was a thing of the past. Unfortunately, very few homes had freezers, so frozen food use languished for a decade.

FRESH FOOD

Vitamins had been discovered in the 1910s, but didn't become important in home cooking for many decades. *The Gun Club Cookbook*, 1930, argued that "nutritional knowledge is the enemy of pleasure."

But technological knowledge changed America's outlook on food. In her 1996 update to her book on *Women and Cooking at the Turn of The Century*, Laura Shapiro recounts an experience she had several years earlier in a panel on American cooking, during which she was making her point that nobody is cooking anymore. Then another panelist interjected that supermarkets are full of fresh food, and people are buying it every day. That panelist was Julia Child, whose *Mastering the Art of French Cooking* dominated the concept of gourmet cooking after its publication in 1961.

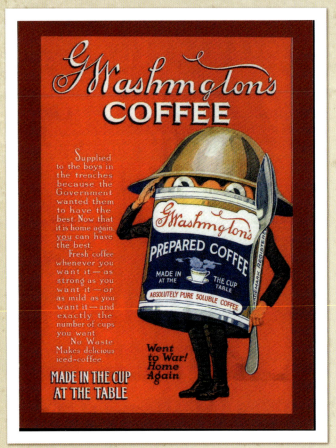

Coffee unavailable. Instant is born.

Secretary's Minutes, October 14, 1943
The officers had an earlier meeting and told us of more rationing by the government and butter is at a premium, let alone gasoline, meat and all that blue stamps buy as well as red ones. The tables were decorated with lovely doilies and silver and even red roses – hard to get in war days. The hostess in these days of rationing went further with her own coupons than we can go as winter comes on. She presented a salad ring mold with heavy cream and crushed pineapple in it, and around it fruits fresh and canned which had been well basted in what tasted like honest to goodness olive oil – maybe not. Hot rolls with plenty of now-precious butter and such good rhubarb and orange conserve, a plentiful relish dish and coffee. No points for coffee now.

Secretary's Minutes, February 25, 1943
Spanish chicken, slaw with grapefruit and an unusual dressing, pineapple ice box cake. The Club received a request to sponsor some Victory Gardening: what seeds to buy and best to buy, etc. The Club decided to refer the request to the Garden Club or the Farm Bureau. There was more discussion about menus since no one has points to spare. Menus will be entirely from non-rationed food. Decision to send $25 to Art Association for the new gallery, and $25 to the Red Cross.

Secretary's Minutes. October 12, 1944
Since beef is almost a thing of the past, in a time of food and gas rationing, the club will continue to meet only once a month.

Secretary's Minutes. December 4, 1944
Christmas Charity gifts will go to Phyllis Wheatley Children's Home and the Home for the Aged.

Secretary's Minutes. January 11, 1945
Menu: Tuna fish loaf with mushroom sauce, tomato aspic, and frozen asparagus salad, French bread, ice box cake with whipped cream garnished with candied fruit. Since rationing seems to be on everything since Christmas, and all meats take more points than ever, every member must bring one red point to every meeting.

Secretary's Minutes. May 24, 1945
Membership having been diminished by death, sickness, and more or less permanent absences due to war, we discussed possible new members. Names were suggested, but were doubtful in this time of practically no household help.

Secretary's Minutes, November 6, 1947
The menu served was escalloped crab meat in shells, corn pudding, glazed red apples, biscuits with orange marmalade topping, gingerbread with lemon sauce and whipped cream, coffee. New yearbooks were distributed and a discussion of the contents followed. As the Club has not had a yearbook for several years, it was much appreciated.

Secretary's Minutes, March 4, 1948
Happy Days! Menu: Baked ham circles topped with pineapple rings, crisp potatoes with horseradish sauce, green vegetable salad with tomato, asparagus, artichoke hearts, carrots and radishes with ranch dressing, cinnamon rolls, orange angel pie with fresh strawberries and whipped cream.

Secretary's Minutes, May 6, 1948
Picnic. The day was lovely in the country and the dining room table was resplendent with a centerpiece of red and white peonies from the garden. The following menu was served: baked ham with horseradish sauce, Boston baked beans in a pot, potato salad, spiced peaches, and cottage cheese. A relish plate was passed, also rolls and strawberry preserves. For dessert we had lemon sherbet and angel food cake with coffee. In the business meeting the Club happily agreed to resume meeting twice a month beginning in October.

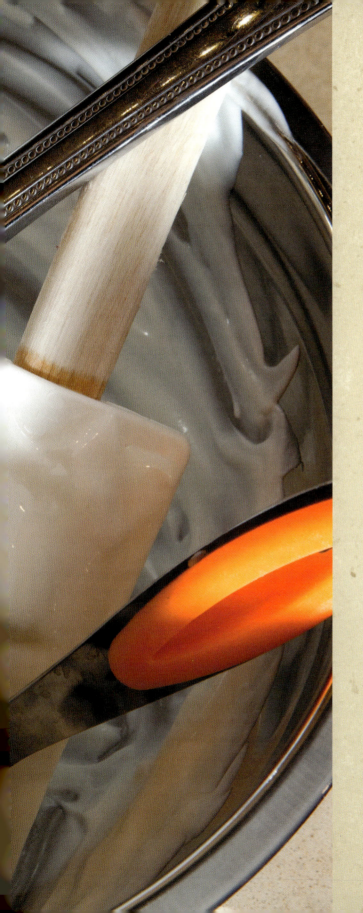

5

AMERICAN COOKING 1960 – 2018

Julia Child published *Mastering the Art of French Cooking* in 1961. While her book did not turn ordinary American cooks into French cooks, it did help to establish food as a sophisticated new topic. Her book identified her audience. "This is a book for the servantless American cook who can be unconcerned on occasion with budgets, waistlines, time schedules, children's meals, the parent-chauffeur-den-mother syndrome." With the phrase "on occasion" she and her coauthors set the book apart from the daily tasks of food preparation. The recipes were complicated and took time and patience. Americans did not want to be French cooks. Instead, the book helped American cooks perform more varied social activities.

BEING AN AMATEUR-PRO IN THE KITCHEN

After reading Child's book, Mary Cantwell wrote in her memoir, *Manhattan When I Was Young*, my dinner parties grew grander. The trick was to be a lady in the dining room, yet an amateur-pro in the kitchen.

On television, Julia Child offered sophistication without stuffiness. She particularly emphasized the notion of fun in the kitchen. Julia Child dropped things, she made mistakes and she chatted in a friendly and humorous way that endeared her to American audiences. She single-handedly made the whisk a must-have kitchen tool.

MENUS

The minutes of the cooking club during this period reflect the expanded world of Wichita women. The menus grew more complicated, the recipes more inclusive of unusual ingredients, and there was more experimentation with spices and fresh vegetables. In other words, club members were being American about their cooking. They began showing individualism, exploration and increased skills.

Nevertheless, angel food cake was served at least once every year. Sometimes it came with frosting containing crushed Heath bars, melding tradition with commercially produced foods.

In 1966 and 1967 more than half of all luncheon salads were gelatin molds. One frequent salad was tomato aspic with avocado or asparagus.

Oysters, the most popular main dish in the early years, had dropped off the menus, and sweetbreads were seldom featured. Individual dishes were often named for someone specific: "Ruby White Dilly Bread" and "Grandmother Garst" soup, among others.

Significantly, in the 1970s Perfection Salad was still making the occasional appearance in menus.

One menu featured dried beef and artichoke hearts in special sauce over Rice Chex – an example of the synthesis of home cooking and commercially prepared foods.

A NAME OF HER OWN

A significant change happened with the Secretary's Minutes from October 14, 1965! Since the very first meeting, TACC members had always been identified by their husband's names. (Mrs. B.H. Campbell, Mrs. E.R. Spangler) Their given names, or first names, were never mentioned, even in the minutes, which might otherwise have been perceived as friendly and personal. The impression is that these women even addressed each other using their husband's names. Some current members still view this format as "what's proper," and names are listed that way in the club directory.

Still, when Sally Cardwell was secretary, members were suddenly being called by their first names in the minutes. There is no mention of whether this big shift was actually discussed by the members, but the change has been followed in the minutes ever since.

The 90th Anniversary, December 1981

Nancy Frazier, Dean Ross, Mary Webster, Sally Cardwell, Alys Tatlock, Betty Foulston, Frances Willis, Shirley Shelton, Mary Garst, Georgia Lilleston, Mary Kennedy, Norma Van Aiken, Ruby White, Eleanor Kincaid, Jayne Mills, Barbara Gardner, Winifred Fisher, Jeanne Yankey

Secretary's Minutes, December 10, 1981
The main table was beautiful with the large epergne with Christmas decorations. At each place was a red and green package containing homemade fudge. The menu: Chicken Almond Casserole, Raspberry-Cranberry Molded Salad, Rum-Chocolate Mousse, Blueberry Muffins with Sugar Coating. The president noted that the club is 90 years old today, and read the minutes of the first meeting.

Secretary's Minutes, October 10, 1991
A very special celebration was held in the home of Eleanor Kinkaid. . . . Our cooking club was established in the year 1891, making it, in 1991, the oldest existing club in Wichita. In honor of such a memorable birthday, the Kinkaids had moved large furniture out of the living room so that 24 members could all be seated at round tables in the Kinkaid's spacious living room. The tables were covered with beautiful white cloths and circled with white chairs. The china and crystal on each table was different. In the center of each table was a large crystal bowl containing a striking arrangement of bittersweet and tiny lilies. We were all surprised and intrigued by the fact that two tiny goldfish were swimming among the flowers in each bowl. Souvenir menus were presented to each member.

Secretary's minutes, November 9, 1972
Chicken and Mushroom crepes, Perfection Salad, broccoli with Hollandaise Sauce, Coffee Cream Pie.

Secretary's Minutes, October 7, 1992
The centerpieces were most appropriate for the crisp and windy fall day. They were made of bittersweet, ivy and plume grass arranged in large copper pots. At each place were napkins tied with several strands of raffia and a sprig of bittersweet. The Cooking Club members were delighted to be served a very unique and delicious Greek luncheon, consisting of the following unusual menu items: Grape leaves, which were passed before we were seated, Greek feta chicken. Phyllo spinach triangles, tabbouleh, humus with pita bread, and for dessert – Kataifi – a nut-filled pastry. What a treat! Of course, we were all impressed by the ingenuity of our hostesses.

Secretary's Minutes, March 8, 1990
Jeanne's spacious new home with its beautiful antique china accents is always a delight to experience. We were treated with the unique experience of observing her daughter's exquisite miniatures. A refreshing bean salad was served on a glorious purple cabbage leaf, accompanied with creamed mushrooms on toast. The dessert of Baked Pears surrounded by puff pastry in a light wine sauce was magnificent. Note: Current members still rave about the delicious Baked Pear dessert served at this luncheon. It was a collaboration between Mary Aikins, a member, and her daughter, Anne White.

ENTERTAINING THIS CLUB IS NOT EASY

All of the current members of the Club confess to feelings of nervousness about pulling off the perfect luncheon. Those who have been members for a while have their own private lists of suppliers they can count on. They plan weeks ahead so they can order online if necessary. In addition, they are all keepers of files of old recipes, new recipes, favorites, etc. Naturally, some have more sophisticated filing systems than others, but they can all pull out the recipe booklets the club began requiring hostesses to furnish at each luncheon. There is a decorative cover that lists the date, the hostess names and the menu. With the increased availability and quality of cellphones with cameras, the booklets now often include photos of the food or the season.

THE 100TH ANNIVERSARY

In 2018, members of the club still like to talk about the 100th event. One reason is a great fondness for Eleanor Kinkaid, who went to such a lot of trouble to seat everyone together in her home. Mrs. Kinkaid has a delicious sense of humor, so, of course, on her tables, goldfish were swimming in the centerpiece bowls.

Eleanor Kinkaid

Written by Kathleen Kelly of *The Wichita Eagle*, "The meal began with a simple golden bouillon served in clear glass punch cups. Floating in the warm broth was whipped cream sprinkled with Jane's Crazy-Mixed-Up Salt. The 100th anniversary salad was waiting on plates for the chicken breasts in phyllo pastry to come from the ovens. Dessert plates later were filled with slices of a rich chocolate mousse garnished with raspberry puree and fresh raspberries. . . . 'Hostessing this club takes a good committee and a patient husband,' said Eleanor Kinkaid."

Secretary's Minutes, May 10, 1990
It was an "Event." . . . an authentic Italian luncheon. . . When we can leave Cooking Club in laughter after a delightful afternoon this is the place to be. Many individual courses were served, each a delight. The salad was cold and crisp – a sliver of cantaloupe carefully ripened since Monday, was enveloped with thin, delicate prosciutto ordered from New York. The cheese Manicotti with Marinara Sauce with a touch of basil was superb. The bread toasted with butter, olive oil and Parmesan Cheese and a harmony of spices was a delight. I can hardly spell Zabaglione let alone pronounce it, but served over carefully quartered perfectly ripened strawberries (I know because this was one of my duties) it was a perfect harmony of color as well as flavor. A delightful cookie was unwrapped carefully so we could later learn a new trick. . . . The wrapper was carefully rolled, then set afire with a match. It floated into the air. We were all amazed.

Secretary's Minutes, January 10, 1991
It was a terribly icy and dreary day, made cheery and warm with lovely fires in two fireplaces. The menu was delightful, served on 100-year-old china: Baked chicken breast stuffed with spinach in puff pastry with Béchamel Sauce, grapefruit, avocado and apple salad with fruit salad dressing. Bran muffins, sand plum jelly, and chocolate ice cream in cups.

Secretary's Minutes, November 13, 2003
The Thursday Afternoon Cooking Club met for a very elegant English Tea. Jodie Mason, Geri Jabara and Penny Moss were co-hostesses. The tea table was beautifully set with gleaming silver and a lovely soup tureen filled with Italian ceramic flowers. Sherry and sparkling apple cider were served to the members when they first arrived. The menu consisted of tea sandwiches made with chicken chutney, smoked salmon and cucumbers; scones with clotted cream, strawberry preserves with sour cream and brown sugar, elegant pumpkin cake and Millionaire's shortbread. Cashews were on the able as well as Earl Grey tea and Hazelnut coffee.

Secretary's Minutes, December 14, 2000
A festive holiday mood prevailed as the group met and mingled on the main floor to sip on cran-champagne cocktails. The finally-final presidential election was the main topic of conversation. The consensus was that Kansas' evolution controversy was no match for Florida's dimples and chads. The menu was: ham roll-ups, mixed greens and goat cheese salad, meringue shells with chocolate and candied cranberries.

BACK ROW Velma Wallace, Betty Meneh NEXT ROW Mary Aikins, Nancy Brammer, Becky Ritchey
NEXT ROW Marilyn Wells, Libby Seymour Marshall, Melody Eby NEXT ROW Janet Buckley, Penny Moss
NEXT ROW Margaret Houston, Liz Enoch, Trudy Haag, Geri Jabara, Georgia Chandler, Dodie Seymour, Chris Kubik
FRONT ROW Jackie Davis, Jeanne Yankey, Genie Reed

DISCOVERED BY THE NEW YORK TIMES

It happened, as these things sometimes do, that a member's son had a friend who had a friend who knew the food writer for *The New York Times*. The cooking club and its age caught the fancy of the writer, and she came to Wichita to check it out. Her story appeared in *The Wichita Eagle*, and memorably, in the *Times*.

A LASTING LUNCH IN WICHITA

Kim Severson, *The New York Times*, April 22, 2015 – "Wichita, Kansas – Texas cattle, Turkey Red Wheat and Pizza Hut all helped build this city on the plains. And in its own quiet way, so has the Thursday Afternoon Cooking Club. For the past 124 years, its members have cooked through generations of culinary trends both excellent and unfortunate, holding together what is said to be the oldest continually operating club devoted to what its founders called the exchange of ideas in cooking and domestic science. . . . Gracious entertaining is a key component . . . but a certain degree of culinary exploration also matters. Members share tips on a new butcher or finding ingredients they may not have heard of before. . . . Over the generations, cooking club members have stood witness to births and deaths and marriage troubles. They have looked out for one another and their shared history. 'There just comes a time in life,' said Margaret Houston. . . . 'when your grandmother's recipes start to matter and you realize it is your job to protect them.' "

Secretary's Minutes, April 9, 2015
The Thursday Afternoon Cooking Club met in the home of Barb Mohney with Nancy Brammer and Lou Ann Ritchie acting as co-hostesses. Joining us for a spring luncheon in the country was our much anticipated guest, Kim Severson, food writer for *The New York Times*. The conversation was lively as we greeted Kim and chatted over a glass of sparkling Naveran Cava. Spring was celebrated in the décor as well as in the menu. The crisp white and soft blue linens with crystal chargers were highlighted by floral arrangements of traditional farm favorites . . . sunflowers, hydrangeas and iris. . . . Melody Moore presented Kim with a gift on behalf of the Club, and Kim said a few words.

ELEGANT AMERICAN COOKING EVOLVES

In January 2008, then President Chris Kubik shared an article she had read about the popularity in France of ready-to-go crusts for tarts, pies, quiche, etc. "So much," she said "for the notion that all French cooks do everything from scratch." The discovery that stores in France were actually offering – and really selling – ready-made crusts was a shocker. Premade and packaged crusts might actually reflect a trend in France toward American-style cooking. Imagine that. Perhaps there is now true globalism in cooking as in other things, like finance and politics.

The demonstrations at meetings may have stopped, but TACC members are still adopting all the basic new equipment and gadgets. Their kitchens have blenders, food processors, microwaves, nonstick pots and pans, plus espresso coffee makers and ice cream machines. They may use induction cooking and spray their pans with butter-flavored PAM. They sometimes make their own cheese, and sometimes buy it in a spray can. When a member discovers a nifty new gadget, others rush to buy it, also.

Cooking Club members pay attention to calories, but they still favor a decadent dessert. They served kale salads when it was popular to do so, but they return occasionally to gelatin salads, or congealed salads, as they were once called.

Club members love to recall and describe spectacular dishes served in years past. They rave about the puff pastry creations members have created. They talk about the fluffy white coconut Christmas pie with sparklers on top, and the crystalized snowflakes made to adorn a delectable dessert. And everyone has a favorite chocolate dessert.

Members believe in cooking from scratch. They also believe in time-saving devices and sometimes turn to shortcuts like frozen puff pastry. Cooking club home life has changed with the rest of the culture. Generations ago, only women did the shopping and cooking. Today men share some of the tasks, and members rejoice in the foods their husbands like to make.

Thursday Afternoon Cooking Club members love to be engaged with food, as cooks and as consumers. More than a chore, cooking is now a choice, and they are more food literate now than ever before, reading labels for calories, vitamins and additives. For all these years, they have been discussing, learning, teaching and questioning everything there is to know about food. And still they love it!

The club motto, "Health, Strength, Happiness," is as appropriate today as when it was adopted in 1891.

6

TASTES OF THE MEDITERRANEAN

SPARKLING POMEGRANATE
COCKTAIL WITH ST. GERMAIN

EGGPLANT YUKHNEE

CITRUS AND
POMEGRANATE SALAD

BAGUETTE
WITH ZA'ATAR

LEBANESE RICE

NAMOURA SEMOLINA HONEY
LEMON SYRUP CAKE

Gretchen Andeel

I married into a large Lebanese family in Wichita, where the Lebanese community has made a huge impact on the city. Lebanese cooking is often a family affair, with individuals adding and subtracting some of the most diverse flavorings in the world. The dense aromas of the food as it cooks are unmatched anywhere except in the myriad dishes from other Middle Eastern countries. I love to fix the Eggplant Yukhnee because it can be made ahead and frozen, and everybody seems to love it.

Lou Ann Ritchie

I am part of an extended family — more than 115 Ritchies in all — and we like gathering in various groupings several times a year. It's a good thing I love to cook! The salad we selected for today's luncheon can accompany any entrée from fish to fowl, and I can dress it up, as I did today, with Mediterranean touches like the Pomegranate perils.

Candace Stultz

My background is in design. I lean toward recipes and foods that look beautiful. Lemon is such a popular flavor in Mediterranean cooking that we searched for exactly the right dessert to end the meal with delight. And, even a novice baker has no need to fear tackling this lovely golden brown cake with a very delicate, heady aroma.

FIRST TACC MEETING OF THE YEAR – 127 YEARS OLD AND COUNTING

It's a PARTY, and the members of the Thursday Afternoon Cooking Club are gathering – just as they have done for the past 127 years. For eight months of the year, on the second Thursday, there is a TACC luncheon in Wichita served by three members. The hostesses carefully plan the menu, test recipes, cook the food and plan elegant tables for dining in the home of one of the hostesses.

Today's luncheon has a Mediterranean flair borne out through the food and table decorations. The meal today is preceded by glasses of Sparkling Pomegranate Cocktail, and a beautiful tray of Cucumber Lebne Bites. The aperitif is a relatively new addition to the TACC luncheons. Within the past 20 years, more and more of the hostesses have turned to offering a simple drink, usually with sparkling wine, before sitting down for lunch. For most of the 127 years, however, the aperitif, usually champagne, was reserved for very special occasions.

The house is filled with the inviting aromas of the spice-laden Middle Eastern kitchen. Soon all 24 members are seated at the tables. The hostesses serve at table in the traditional way – serve from the left, clear from the right. The luncheon is, predictably, delicious, because all three hostesses are acclaimed cooks and hostesses.

In the kitchen is a helper, paid by the hostess and an indispensable part of today's TACC luncheons. She can do anything assigned to her in the kitchen, but long-standing rules prevent her from stepping into the dining room. Sometimes, as she does today, she comes into the living room to serve aperitifs and pass appetizers.

SPARKLING POMEGRANATE COCKTAIL WITH ST. GERMAIN

SERVES A CROWD
1 PART CHILLED POMEGRANATE JUICE
1 PART CHILLED PROSECCO
1 PART CHILLED SODA WATER
SPLASH OF ST. GERMAIN FOR EACH SERVING

Mix everything in a pitcher or individual glasses with ice and serve immediately. St. Germain is a sweet liquor made with elderflowers.

EGGPLANT YUKHNEE

1 LARGE ONION, DICED
⅓ C RENDERED BUTTER OR CREAMERY BUTTER
1 LB LEAN AND WELL-TRIMMED COURSE-GROUND TOP-ROUND BEEF
½ TSP CINNAMON
¼ TSP LEBANESE 7-SPICE OR ALLSPICE
2 TSP SALT, DIVIDED
¼ TSP PEPPER
2 CLOVES GARLIC, MINCED
¼ C PINE NUTS
2 LARGE, DARK EGGPLANTS
½ C MELTED BUTTER, RENDERED BUTTER OR OLIVE OIL
1 6-OZ CAN TOMATO PASTE
2 TO 3 C WATER
¼ C LEMON JUICE
SALT AND PEPPER TO TASTE

Preheat oven to 350°F. Lightly grease 9x12x2-inch baking dish. Sauté onion in butter and add ground meat, spices, 1 teaspoon salt and pepper. Cook until done. Add pine nuts and half of garlic. Set aside to cool. Peel the eggplants in stripes and slice eggplants into round slices ¾ inches think. Brush butter or oil on both sides of rounds and place on a greased cookie sheet. Brown on both sides in oven broiler and place eggplant slices in baking dish. Put some meat mixture on each slice and press. Add tomato paste diluted in enough water (2-3 cups) to cover eggplant slices. Add lemon juice and remaining garlic, 1 teaspoon salt and pepper to taste, and pour over eggplant. Bake 35 to 40 minutes until bubbly. Serve over Lebanese rice.

A Planning Meeting

Well ahead of the meeting, the hostesses gather to look at recipes and meal plans. Before the TACC meeting date they will have tested every recipe they are considering. They will consult on flowers and table décor. Each hostess will prepare some portion of the menu and bring it to the luncheon.

CITRUS AND POMEGRANATE SALAD

SALAD
- ½ HEAD ICEBERG LETTUCE, TORN INTO BITE-SIZED PIECES
- ½ HEAD BIBB LETTUCE, TORN INTO BITE-SIZED PIECES
- 2 C CELERY, CHOPPED
- 2 T FRESH PARSLEY, CHOPPED FINE
- 4 GREEN ONIONS, WITH TOPS, SLICED, DRAINED
- 2 11-OZ CANS MANDARIN ORANGES, DRAINED
- PERILS OF ONE POMEGRANATE
- ½ C SLIVERED ALMONDS
- ¼ C BUTTER

DRESSING
- 1 TSP SALT
- PINCH PEPPER
- ½ TSP TABASCO SAUCE
- ¼ C SUGAR
- ¼ C TARRAGON VINEGAR
- ½ C SALAD OIL

Salad Combine the lettuces, celery, parsley, green onions, mandarin oranges and pomegranate perils in a salad bowl. Toast almonds in butter in a 350°F oven, just until golden, watching carefully.

Dressing Combine dressing ingredients, mixing well, and combine with salad. Sprinkle toasted almonds over top and serve at once.

Note Pomegranate perils may be spread on a cookie sheet and frozen in a single layer, then transferred to a plastic bag for storage in a freezer. This makes them available in the off seasons. Just toss them into the salad and they defrost immediately. Perils already extracted from the pomegranate are available at most grocery stores for a while after the middle of October.

BAGUETTE WITH ZA'ATAR

1 BAGUETTE
SCANT C OF EXTRA-VIRGIN OLIVE OIL

ZA'ATAR SPICE BLEND
4 T CHOPPED FRESH OREGANO
4 T SUMAC
4 T GROUND CUMIN
4 T SESAME SEEDS
4 TSP KOSHER SALT
4 TSP FRESHLY GROUND
   BLACK PEPPER

Slice one baguette into ½-inch slices. Mix 1 cup Za'atar Spice Blend with scant cup of extra-virgin olive oil.

Preheat oven to 350°F. Spread Za'atar mixture on each slice of baguette and place on a parchment-lined baking sheet. Bake for 5 minutes.

Can be made 2 weeks ahead. Store airtight at room temperature. You can find Za'atar and Sumac at Middle Eastern markets, specialty foods stores and wholespice.com.

LEBANESE RICE

2 C UNCLE BEN'S CONVERTED RICE
   (PARBOILED RICE)
¾ C VERMICELLI, CRUSHED INTO
   ½-INCH PIECES
2 T RENDERED BUTTER OR OLIVE OIL
3 C BOILING WATER
1 T SALT

Wash rice and cover with hot water to stand for 15 minutes. In a deep saucepan brown vermicelli in butter. Drain rice, add to vermicelli and stir for 2 minutes. Add boiling water and bring to a hard boil. Add salt, cover and simmer until moisture is absorbed, about 20 minutes. Remove from stove and let sit about 5 minutes. Garnish with pine nuts browned in butter.

Serves 6. This rice can be turned into a buttered casserole and reheated, covered, about 20 minutes at 300°F.

NAMOURA
SEMOLINA HONEY LEMON SYRUP CAKE

CAKE
2 C FINE SEMOLINA
1 C DESICCATED COCONUT (SHREDDED)
½ C SUGAR
1 TSP BAKING SODA
⅔ C MELTED BUTTER OR GHEE
1 C MILK

SYRUP
1½ C SUGAR
1½ C WATER
1 T LIME JUICE OR 2 T LEMON JUICE
2 T HONEY

PREHEAT THE OVEN TO 345°F

Cake In a large bowl mix together all the dry ingredients. Add the butter and milk and stir until well combined. Pour into a buttered, shallow, medium-sized oven-proof dish. Bake for 30 minutes or until golden brown on the top.

Syrup In a medium sauce pan, place the sugar and water on low heat and stir until the sugar dissolves completely. Increase the heat to medium and bring to a vigorous boil, cooking until it coats the back of a spoon or reduces by about one-third (or until it reaches 220°F). Stir in the lime juice and allow to cool. Once cooled, stir in the honey.

Assemble Allow the cake to cool for about 10 minutes, and then cut it into small squares or diamonds. Carefully pour the syrup over the cake. It is a lot of syrup, but the cake will gradually absorb all of it. This might take a couple of hours. Dress up the cake by sprinkling with desiccated coconut or blanched almonds. Serve at room temperature.

TACC Meeting

Following luncheon, the members gather for the business meeting, part of which is always a review of the menu and recipes. On this day, Gretchen talks about Lebanese cooking and reminds everyone that spices for Middle Eastern foods are very easily available in Wichita. There is much appreciation for all of the foods offered today.

7

MID-CENTURY REVISITED

GEORGIA'S
CHEESE SOUFFLÈ

CRANBERRY SALAD

CHOCOLATE
MARSHMALLOW PIE

GEORGIA'S CHEESE SOUFFLÈ

1 C SCALDED MILK
1 C SOFT STALE BREAD CRUMBS
¼ LB MILK CHEESE (VELVEETA)
    CUT IN SMALL PIECES (1 C)
1 T BUTTER
½ TSP SALT
½ TSP DRY MUSTARD
3 EGG YOLKS
3 EGG WHITES
BUTTER
PARMESAN CHEESE,
    FINELY GRATED

Preheat oven to 350°F.

Mix first six ingredients, cook over low heat until smooth, stirring with a fork. Beat yolks in a medium bowl until lemon colored. Add cheese mixture to the yolks. Making sure there is no egg yolk in the whites, in a clean bowl, beat egg whites until stiff. Fold whites into cheese mixture.

Butter a 1-quart baking dish with tall sides (or fill four 10-ounce ramekins). Sprinkle dish with Parmesan cheese to cover the bottom. Ladle or pour mixture into baking dish. Bake 25-30 minutes. Top should be golden brown and filling should be soft.

CRANBERRY SALAD

1 PKG RASPBERRY JELL-O
1 CAN WHOLE CRANBERRY SAUCE (14 OZ)
1 8-OZ CAN PINEAPPLE TIDBITS (USE JUICE IN JELL-O)
1 APPLE, CUT UP
2 STALKS OF CELERY, CUT UP
1 8-OZ CAN MANDARIN ORANGES
½ C CHOPPED PECANS

Heat cranberry sauce to boiling and dissolve Jell-O in it. Add pineapple, apple, celery, oranges and nuts. Pour into a large ring mold or glass dish. Chill several hours.

Serves 6-8.

TACC invites you to revisit the foods the nation loved nearly a century ago.

Georgia Chandler

In high school Georgia Chandler, an honorary member, learned a soufflé recipe that used Velveeta cheese. In that earlier time, Velveeta was a marvelous new cheese, and the taste of this soufflé is undoubtedly Velveeta. The texture is spongy and delicate. Our kitchen testers loved it. In 2006, some TACC members decided to re-create a menu that calls back an older age. The club honored this recipe by choosing it. For three decades in the 1950s to 1980s, salads served at TACC luncheons were made of Jell-O almost half the time. This cranberry salad could have been served then, and it is quite tasty today.

CHOCOLATE MARSHMALLOW PIE

9-INCH COOKED PIE SHELL
1 C SUGAR
8 T (SLIGHTLY ROUNDED) ALL-PURPOSE FLOUR
½ C LESS 2 T COCOA
¼ TSP SALT
2 C WHOLE MILK
14 LARGE MARSHMALLOWS
2 T BUTTER
1 TSP VANILLA
½ C PECANS, CHOPPED (OPTIONAL)
1 PT HEAVY CREAM
3-5 T POWDERED SUGAR
GRATED CHOCOLATE

Directions Mix sugar, flour, salt and cocoa in a heavy medium-sized saucepan. Add milk, stirring it in slowly. Cook over low heat for 5 minutes. Add the marshmallows and cook until thick, stirring constantly as it burns easily. When thickened, stir in butter and vanilla. Add chopped nuts at the end. Let cook. Stir and pour into pie shell. Refrigerate. Top with whipped cream.

Whipped Cream Pour cream into a cold container and whip with cold beaters until starting to become thick. Add powdered sugar to taste. Whip until it forms a mound when dropped from beaters. Add 1 teaspoon vanilla and combine, being careful not to beat too long as it will turn to butter.

Tip The cream should be firm enough to drop big spoonfuls of cream all around the edge and fill the center with more big spoonfuls. Then with the bottom of a spoon, carefully spread the cream to edges of the crust and move the other mounds around to fill in the middle, leaving peaks of the whipped cream all over the pie. You can then take a chocolate square or chocolate bar, and grate a little onto a piece of waxed paper and sprinkle the grated chocolate over the whipped cream.

Sondra Robison

Sondra found a pie recipe she likes, one that uses marshmallows to gel a rich chocolate filling. Marshmallow desserts were all the rage after the Second World War. This recipe tastes very up to date.

8

COOL AND CASUAL

OPEN-FACED BAKED
CRAB CROISSANT

✧

TOMATO ASPIC
SALAD

✧

S'MORES COFFEE AND
FUDGE ICE CREAM CAKE
WITH FUDGE SAUCE

OPEN-FACED BAKED CRAB CROISSANT

- ½ C LIGHT MAYONNAISE
- ½ TSP DRIED DILL WEED
- ½ TSP GARLIC POWDER
- ⅛ TSP CAYENNE PEPPER
- ⅔ LB CRAB MEAT (CANNED OR FROZEN), DRAINED (10.6 OZ)
- ½ C SHREDDED CHEDDAR CHEESE
- ½ C SHREDDED MONTEREY JACK CHEESE
- 1 C CANNED ARTICHOKES, DRAINED AND CHOPPED
- ¼ C FINELY CHOPPED CELERY
- 8 LARGE CROISSANTS, SPLIT
- FINELY GRATED PARMESAN CHEESE
- A PINCH OF PAPRIKA

Preheat oven to 375°F.

Combine first nine ingredients. Spread mixture on bottom half of croissant. Add a sprinkling of Parmesan cheese and a pinch of paprika. Place on a baking sheet and bake until heated through – 15 minutes. Spread upper half of croissant with soft butter and toast lightly.

Serves 8, one croissant per person.

Notes Our testing kitchen tried a variety of crab meats. Frozen tastes freshest. Bumble Bee canned crab was white and tastes very good, but it was flakey and disappeared into the salad. We preferred bites of crab, such as hearty pasteurized crab. When buying crab meat, pay attention to DR (drained) weight on the label, and be aware that when you drain it, the crab will drop in weight. Bumble Bee DR WT 4.25 ounces, came out 3.8 ounces after we drained it. So, 3 cans was just right.

Baking Croissants

In our testing kitchen we used purchased croissants, but making your own is not difficult. All that is necessary is good technique. Follow a recipe for making a simple dough. Roll it out to 10 inches square and chill it. Make a 5-inch square of chilled butter by beating it flat. Place the butter square in the center of the dough and fold the sides in to cover it. Roll it out and fold again, and again, laminating the butter within the dough. As the cold butter is incorporated throughout the dough you are creating the structure that will make your croissants crisp and flaky. Once ready, cut the dough into triangles, roll it up and cover with an egg wash. Let them rise in a warm place for 1½ hours and then bake at 425°F for 8-10 minutes. Baking croissants was the subject of a number of demonstrations presented to the club over the years.

TOMATO ASPIC SALAD

ASPIC
1 3-OZ PKG LEMON JELL-O
1 C PLAIN TOMATO JUICE
1 C SPICY TOMATO JUICE
1¾ TSP GRATED ONION
1 TSP HORSERADISH
½ C FINELY DICED CELERY
1 TSP WORCESTERSHIRE
¼ C SLICED STUFFED OLIVES
1 AVOCADO, CHOPPED

DRESSING (OPTIONAL)
1½ C LIGHT MAYONNAISE
3-OZ PKG SOFT PHILADELPHIA
   CREAM CHEESE WITH CHIVES
½ TSP GRATED ONION
SQUIRT OF LEMON JUICE

Aspic Heat the tomato juices and dissolve Jell-O in them. Cool. When slightly thickened but not set, add onion, horseradish and Worcestershire; mix. Add celery, avocado and olives. Refrigerate until set in 8x8-inch glass dish. If using molds, spray lightly with oil.

Dressing Beat dressing until smooth and add a dollop before serving.

Serves 8.

Aspic Salad

Aspic has been served frequently throughout the years for the club. Just seeing it reminds club members of a dearly loved former member who was truly fond of it, and served it often. She loved the shine of it, and the many forms it could be given. And, it was red. What could be better for a buffet table than a red molded salad?

S'MORES COFFEE AND FUDGE ICE CREAM CAKE

ICE CREAM CAKE
16 WHOLE GRAHAM CRACKERS
1 C WHOLE ALMONDS, TOASTED
3 T SUGAR
1 7-OZ JAR MARSHMALLOW CREME
2 C MINIATURE MARSHMALLOWS
1 C WHIPPING CREAM
½ C LIGHT CORN SYRUP
10 OZ BITTERSWEET CHOCOLATE
½ C UNSALTED BUTTER, MELTED
1½ QUARTS COFFEE ICE CREAM, SOFTENED UNTIL SPREADABLE

TOPPING
1 7-OZ JAR MARSHALLOW CREME
2 C MINIATURE MARSHMALLOWS

FUDGE SAUCE
1 C WHIPPING CREAM
½ C LIGHT CORN SYRUP
10 OZ BITTERSWEET CHOCOLATE

Preheat oven to 350°F.

Layer One Finely grind graham crackers, toasted almonds and 3 tablespoons sugar in food processor. Add ½ cup melted butter, process mixture until moist crumbs form. Press graham cracker mixture onto bottom and up sides of 9-inch diameter spring form pan with 1¾-inch sides. Bake crust until edges are golden, about 12 minutes. Cool crust completely. (Best made a day or so ahead.)

Layer Two Spread 2 cups softened ice cream atop cake in baking pan. Freeze. Spoon ¾ cup cooled fudge sauce over. Freeze until sauce is just set, at least 10 minutes. Refrigerate or freeze remaining ice cream as necessary to prevent melting.

Layer Three Repeat layering with 2 cups ice cream, then ¾ cup sauce. Freeze until sauce is just set. Spread remaining 2 cups ice cream over. Cover and freeze overnight. Refrigerate remaining fudge sauce. Preheat broiler. Place cake in pan on baking sheet. A kitchen torch could be used instead of the broiler.

Topping Spread marshmallow creme over top of cake. Sprinkle miniature marshmallows over top in single layer. Broil just until marshmallows are deep brown, watching closely to prevent burning, about 1 minute. Run knife between pan sides and cake to loosen. Remove pan sides. Cut cake in wedges immediately and serve with warm fudge sauce.

Fudge Sauce Bring cream and corn syrup to boil in heavy medium saucepan. Remove from heat. Chop chocolate, add to cream and whisk until melted and smooth. Refrigerate until cool but still pourable, stirring occasionally, about 45 minutes.

Serves 10-12.

Ruthie Gillespie

I love to entertain, and this cake is certainly a party cake – maybe even a birthday cake. Creating a unique and delicious menu to pair with an imaginative tablescape is great fun for me. I love curling up with an interesting cookbook to explore intriguing recipes and find something new to play with.

9

MAKING MEMORIES

SHELLFISH CREPES
IN WINE-CHEESE SAUCE

BAKED RICE
(RECIPE NOT INCLUDED)

ROASTED PEAR SALAD
WITH CANDIED PECANS
AND APPLE-GRAPE VINAIGRETTE

EGG NOG ICE CREAM

EASY NO-COOK
CHOCOLATE MOCHA ICE CREAM

GRANDMA PEARL'S
ICE BOX COOKIES

MAKING MEMORIES

Fawn McDonough

In regular life, I'm a nurse. In cooking that translates to meticulous adherence to the written recipe, exact measuring and perfect timing – not always possible in the kitchen. But I have a stash of my family's recipes I love to use. Check out the recipe for my Grandma Pearl's Ice Box Cookies.

Trudy Haag

TACC has a tradition of demonstrating tools and techniques for the members, so Fawn and I showed how easy it is to make crepes with a crepe maker. I'm a collector of many things, including beautiful wine glasses.

SHELLFISH CREPES IN WINE-CHEESE SAUCE

WINE-CHEESE SAUCE
YIELD: 4 CUPS
¼ C CORNSTARCH
¼ C MILK
⅓ C SHERRY (OR VERMOUTH)
3 C WHIPPING CREAM
¼ TSP SALT
¼ TSP PEPPER
2 C (8 OZ) SHREDDED SWISS CHEESE

CREPES
4 LARGE EGGS
2 C ALL-PURPOSE FLOUR
¼ C BUTTER OR MARGARINE, MELTED
1 C COLD WATER
1 C COLD MILK
½ TSP SALT

FILLING
½ C BUTTER OR MARGARINE, DIVIDED
2 C CHOPPED COOKED SHRIMP (ABOUT 1 LB)
1 C (8 OZ) FRESH CRAB MEAT
2 GREEN ONIONS, MINCED
¼ C DRY SHERRY (OR VERMOUTH, OR CLAM JUICE)
⅛ TSP SALT
¼ TSP PEPPER
½ T BUTTER OR MARGARINE, MELTED
2 C SHREDDED SWISS CHEESE

GARNISH
SLICED GREEN ONIONS

Sauce Whisk together cornstarch and milk in a small bowl. Bring sherry (or vermouth) to a boil in a large skillet, and cook until reduced to 1 tablespoon. Remove from heat and whisk in cornstarch mixture. Add whipping cream, salt and pepper; cook over medium-high heat, whisking constantly, 2 minutes or until mixture comes to a boil. Boil 1 minute or until thickened. Add Swiss cheese, reduce heat and simmer, whisking constantly, 1 minute, or until sauce is smooth.

Crepes Process all ingredients in a blender or food processor until smooth. Cover and refrigerate 1 hour. Spray PAM on a non-stick omelet pan, and heat until hot. Pour 3 tablespoons batter into skillet, quickly tilting in all directions to cover bottom of skillet. Cook 1 minute or until crepe can be shaken loose. Turn crepe and cook about 30 seconds. Invert onto waxed paper. Repeat with remaining batter.

Filling Melt ¼ cup butter in a large skillet over medium-high heat. Add shrimp, crab and green onions, and sauté for 1 minute. Stir in sherry, salt and pepper. Bring to a boil and cook 7 minutes or until most of liquid is absorbed. Remove from heat and set aside. Drizzle ½ tablespoon melted butter in a 9x13-inch baking dish. Stir 2 cups Wine-Cheese sauce into shrimp mixture. Spoon about 3 tablespoons shrimp mixture down the center of each crepe. Roll up and place seam side down in baking dish. Spoon remaining 2 cups Wine-Cheese Sauce over crepes. Sprinkle with Swiss cheese and dot with remaining ¼ cup butter. Cover and chill for 3 hours. Let stand at room temperature for 30 minutes. Bake at 350°F for 20 minutes or until thoroughly heated. Garnish and serve over baked rice if desired.

24 crepes, serves 12.

ROASTED PEAR SALAD
WITH CANDIED PECANS AND APPLE-GRAPE VINAIGRETTE

SALAD
4 BOSC OR BARTLETT PEARS
SEVERAL SPRIGS FRESH THYME
⅓ C PURE MAPLE SYRUP
⅓ C HONEY
FETA OR GORGONZOLA CHEESE
BABY GREENS
POMEGRANATE SEEDS FOR GARNISH

DRESSING
3 T FROZEN APPLE JUICE CONCENTRATE, THAWED
3 T FROZEN WHITE GRAPE JUICE CONCENTRATE, THAWED
2 T WHITE WINE VINEGAR
1 TSP MINCED SHALLOT
SPRIG FRESH THYME
¾ C VEGETABLE OIL

CANDIED PECANS
1 C CHOPPED PECANS
¼ C WHITE SUGAR
¼ C BROWN SUGAR
¼ TSP EACH OF CINNAMON, NUTMEG AND ALLSPICE
PINCH OF CAYENNE
1 EGG WHITE, WHIPPED UNTIL FROTHY

Preheat oven to 400°F. Peel and core pears, and cut each in half. Make crosswise slices into each pear about ⅜ inch apart, being careful not to cut all the way through. Fan the slices a bit so the honey mixture will seep in between slices. Combine the syrup and honey. Line a cookie sheet with parchment paper. Place pear half atop a sprig of thyme on the parchment. Liberally brush on the honey mixture over the pears and into the grooves. Roast 10-15 minutes.

Remove from oven and repeat basting. Return to oven and bake until soft when gently poked with a fork. (Time varies with the ripeness of pears, but generally about 10 minutes more.) You will want to serve pears warm, so don't bake until about 30 minutes before serving time.

Dressing Mix all ingredients together and let marinate at room temperature for an hour.

Candied pecans Mix together all the sugars, spices and cayenne. With your fingers, dip the nuts in small batches in the egg whites, then roll in the sugar mixture. Spread nuts on a cookie sheet coated with cooking spray. Bake 30 minutes at 325°F, stirring about halfway through.

Assemble Make a bed of baby greens. Place one warm pear half on each. Crumble a little feta or gorgonzola cheese over each and sprinkle with some candied pecans and pomegranate seeds. Drizzle with dressing and serve.

Serves 8.

Margaret Houston

My grandmother, Carrie May Carson, was a member of the cooking club in the 1950s. The joke for me is that I didn't know it until I was already a member, and saw a newspaper clipping with her photo in a club album. She had a reputation in the family as a great cook, and it is a large family of people who all seem to love food and cooking.

EGG NOG ICE CREAM

1 C WHOLE MILK
¼ TSP SALT
7 LARGE EGG YOLKS
¾ C SUGAR
2 C CHILLED HEAVY CREAM
3 T DARK RUM
1 TSP VANILLA
¼ TSP FRESHLY GRATED NUTMEG
 (EXTRA FOR GARNISH IF DESIRED)

Bring milk and salt to boil in a heavy saucepan over moderate heat. Remove from heat. Whisk together yolks and sugar in a bowl, gradually adding ¼ cup hot milk, whisking. Add yolk mixture to milk remaining in the pan in a slow steady stream, whisking and cooking over low heat, stirring constantly with a wooden spoon, until mixture is slightly thickened, coats the back of a spoon, and registers 175°F on a thermometer (approximately 3-5 minutes). Immediately pour through a fine mesh sieve set in a clean bowl. Stir in cream, rum, vanilla and nutmeg. Cover and chill until cold (at least 2 hours).

Freeze in ice cream maker, according to manufacturer's directions. Then transfer to an airtight container and put in freezer to harden, at least 2 hours. Soften slightly in fridge before serving.

EASY NO-COOK CHOCOLATE MOCHA ICE CREAM

1½ C WHOLE MILK
2 C HEAVY CREAM
½ C UNSWEETENED COCOA POWDER
 (GOOD QUALITY AND FRESH)
1 C GRANULATED SUGAR
1 TSP VANILLA EXTRACT
1 TSP COFFEE POWDER (OPTIONAL)

Whisk together milk, cocoa powder and sugar to combine. The sugar and cocoa should be completely dissolved. Stir in heavy cream and vanilla extract.

Refrigerate the chocolate ice cream base for at least 30 minutes before putting it in your ice cream freezer, so it is completely cold. This will help it freeze faster, improving the texture, and allow the cocoa powder to become fully hydrated by the milk and cream.

Give the ice cream base one additional stir and freeze according to the directions for your ice cream freezer. Store in an airtight plastic container in the back of the freezer.

GRANDMA PEARL'S ICE BOX COOKIES

1 LB BUTTER
1 C PACKED BROWN SUGAR
1 C WHITE SUGAR
3 EGGS
1 TSP VANILLA
6 C FLOUR
1 TSP BAKING SODA
3 T HOT WATER
1 LB WHOLE WALNUTS

Cream butter and both sugars until fluffy. Add eggs and vanilla. In a separate bowl mix flour and baking soda. Alternately add 1 tablespoon of hot water, followed by 1-2 cups dry ingredients until all water and flour have been incorporated, ending with dry ingredients. Add walnuts and mix. The cookie dough will be very dense.

Tear four sheets of waxed paper about the length of a cookie sheet. Place ¼ of the dough on each sheet down the length of the rectangle. Pull the long sides together and fold several times to make a long loaf of dough. Fold the ends in and refrigerate overnight. Slice cold dough to desired thickness (approximately ¼ inch). Bake on ungreased pan at 375°F for 10-15 minutes until golden brown. Cool on rack. Each loaf can make 24-36 cookies. Dough freezes well.

Makes 48-65 cookies.

Fawn's Grandma Pearl always had a log of this cookie dough ready to cut and bake, making wonderful memories for a grandchild.

10

CLASSIC CUISINE

ROASTED SHRIMP
AND ORZO

✧

MIXED GREENS
WITH APPLES, CHEDDAR
AND SPICED PECANS

✧

APPLE CRANBERRY
MUFFINS

✧

THE PROSPECT'S
CARROT CAKE

ROASTED SHRIMP AND ORZO

KOSHER SALT
GOOD OLIVE OIL
1½ C ORZO PASTA (RICE-SHAPED PASTA)
½ C FRESHLY SQUEEZED LEMON JUICE (3 LEMONS)
2 TSP FRESHLY GROUND BLACK PEPPER, DIVIDED USE
4 TSP KOSHER SALT, DIVIDED USE
1 T BUTTER (FOR PRE-COOKED SHRIMP)
1 C MINCED SCALLIONS, WHITE AND GREEN PARTS
1 C CHOPPED FRESH DILL
1 C CHOPPED FRESH FLAT-LEAF PARSLEY
25 ASPARAGUS SPEARS, CUT INTO 1-INCH PIECES, BLANCHED FOR 1 MINUTE
½ C FINELY DICED SMALL RED ONION
15 GRAPE TOMATOES, CUT IN HALF
¾ LB GOOD FETA CHEESE, LARGE DICED
2 LBS (16 TO 18 COUNT) SHRIMP, PEELED AND DEVEINED (OR USE SMALLER COOKED SHRIMP)
¾ C PANKO
2 T GRATED PARMESAN CHEESE
1 T SUMMER SAVORY
2 T MELTED BUTTER

Preheat the oven to 400°F.

Orzo To a large pot of boiling, salted water with a splash of oil, add the orzo and simmer for 9 to 11 minutes, stirring occasionally, until it's cooked al dente. Drain and pour into a 3-quart casserole.

Whisk together the lemon juice, ½ cup olive oil, 2 teaspoons salt and 1 teaspoon of pepper. Pour over the hot pasta and stir well.

Add to the orzo the scallions, dill, parsley, asparagus, onion, tomatoes, 2 teaspoons salt and 1 teaspoon pepper. Toss well. Add the feta and stir carefully.

Cooked Shrimp If using pre-cooked shrimp, warm it briefly in a skillet with butter, and add it to the orzo now.

Set aside for 1 hour to allow the flavors to blend, or refrigerate overnight. If refrigerated, taste again for seasonings and bring back to room temperature before serving.

Roasted Shrimp Place the shrimp on a sheet pan, drizzle lightly with olive oil, and sprinkle with salt and pepper. Roast for 5 to 6 minutes, until the shrimp are cooked through. Don't overcook! Place roasted shrimp atop orzo.

Panko Topping Mix together Panko, cheese, savory and butter. Cover orzo and shrimp with Panko topping and brown under broiler.

Serve warm or at room temperature.

MIXED GREENS
WITH APPLES, CHEDDAR AND SPICED PECANS

SALAD
12 C SALAD GREENS (BABY GREENS, ROMAINE AND/OR LEAF LETTUCE)
2 LARGE RED APPLES CUT INTO SLICES
1 C SHREDDED SHARP WHITE CHEDDAR
GARNISH: WITH 1 C SUGARED AND SPICED PECANS AND SHREDDED OR SHAVED CHEDDAR

DRESSING
⅓ C APPLE CIDER VINEGAR
2 TSP DIJON MUSTARD
1 T BROWN SUGAR
1 TSP SALT
1 TSP FRESH THYME LEAVES OR ¼ TSP DRIED THYME
⅛ TSP CAYENNE PEPPER
1 C CANOLA OIL

SPICED PECANS
1 TSP KOSHER SALT
½ TSP GROUND CUMIN
½ TSP CAYENNE PEPPER
½ TSP GROUND CINNAMON
½ TSP DRIED GROUND ORANGE PEEL
1 LB PECAN HALVES
4 T UNSALTED BUTTER
¼ C PACKED LIGHT BROWN SUGAR
2 T PACKED DARK BROWN SUGAR
2 T WATER

Recipe from *Culinary Concepts*.

Combine greens together in a large bowl. Add apples and cheese. Toss with enough dressing to coat greens. To serve, distribute among salad plates. Top with additional cheese and pecans.

Dressing Whisk first six ingredients together in a small bowl. Slowly whisk in oil. Taste and adjust salt and pepper.

Spiced Pecans Line a half sheet pan with parchment paper and set aside. Mix the salt, cumin, cayenne, cinnamon and orange peel together in a small bowl and set aside. Place the nuts in a 10-inch cast iron skillet and set over medium heat. Cook, stirring frequently, for 4 to 5 minutes until they just start to brown and smell toasted. Add the butter and stir until it melts. Add the spice mixture and stir to combine. Once combined, add both sugars and water, stirring until the mixture thickens and coats the nuts, approximately 3 to 4 minutes. Transfer the nuts to the prepared sheet pan and separate them with a fork or spatula. Allow the nuts to cool completely before transferring to an airtight container for storage. Can be stored up to 3 weeks.

Serves 8.

This salad is truly colorful with its red, green and yellow colors. The pecans are spectacular and can be used in many salads or just as a snack.

APPLE CRANBERRY MUFFINS

4 T BUTTER
1 EGG
½ C SUGAR
GRATED RIND OF ONE LARGE ORANGE
½ C FRESH ORANGE JUICE
1 C FLOUR
1 TSP BAKING POWDER
½ TSP BAKING SODA
1 TSP EACH CINNAMON, NUTMEG, ALLSPICE
½ TSP GRATED NUTMEG
½ TSP GROUND ALLSPICE
½ TSP GROUND GINGER
¼ TSP SALT
¾ C APPLE, CORED, PEELED AND DICED
1 C CRANBERRIES
½ C CHOPPED WALNUTS

Recipe online from *The Practical Encyclopedia of Baking*.

Preheat oven to 350°F. Grease 12-cup muffin tin.

Melt butter and cool.

Place egg in mixing bowl and whisk lightly. Add melted butter and combine. Add sugar, orange rind and juice, whisking to blend.

In large bowl sift flour, baking powder, baking soda, spices and salt. Make a well in dry ingredients and pour in egg mixture, stirring to blend. Add apple, cranberries and nuts. Fill cups ¾ full and bake 25-30 minutes.

Serves 12.

THE PROSPECT'S CARROT CAKE

CAKE
1¼ C OIL
2 C SUGAR
2 C ALL-PURPOSE FLOUR
2 TSP BAKING POWDER
2 TSP CINNAMON
1 TSP BAKING SODA
1 TSP SALT
4 EGGS
1 LB CARROTS, PEELED
  AND GRATED
1 C COARSELY CHOPPED PECANS
1 C DARK RAISINS (OPTIONAL)

FILLING
1 C SUGAR
¼ C FLOUR
1 C HEAVY CREAM
¼ C BUTTER
¼ TSP SALT
1 C CHOPPED PECANS
2 TSP VANILLA

FROSTING
4 OZ SHREDDED COCONUT
1 8-OZ PKG CREAM CHEESE,
  ROOM TEMPERATURE
1 C BUTTER, ROOM TEMPERATURE
3 C CONFECTIONER'S SUGAR
1 TSP VANILLA

From The Prospect of Westport Restaurant, Kansas City. This cake is unbelievably dense and delicious. It takes some time to make, because it has filling and frosting, and it has to cool to be split into layers. It is absolutely worth every minute of your time. A fabulous cake!

Preheat oven to 325°F.

Cake Combine oil and sugar in a bowl, beating well. Sift together dry ingredients. Sift half of dry ingredients into sugar mixture, blending well. Sift in remaining dry ingredients alternating with eggs, mixing well after each addition. Stir in carrots, pecans and raisins. Pour into lightly oiled 10-inch tube pan. Bake about 1 hour and 10 minutes. Cool upright in pan.

Filling Combine sugar and flour in small heavy saucepan. Gradually stir in cream. Add butter and salt. Cook over very low heat, stirring frequently, until mixture comes just to a simmer (This may take 30 minutes.) Let simmer 2-3 minutes. Remove from heat and cool to lukewarm. Stir in nuts and vanilla. Cool completely, ideally overnight.

Frosting Toast coconut at 300°F for 10-15 minutes or until lightly browned. Cool. Combine cream cheese and butter in food processor or mixer. Add confectioner's sugar and vanilla and mix until perfectly smooth. Refrigerate if too soft to spread immediately.

Assemble Split cooled cake into three layers. Spread pecan filling between layers, reassembling on cake plate. Frost top and sides, patting toasted coconut onto sides of cake.

Serves 12.

Melody Moore

After an article about our club appeared in *The New York Times*, we realized our archive represented a 125-year food and cooking history of Wichita. I started collecting and organizing as many years of recipes as I could find and created a database to enhance our archive. In the testing kitchen I was handed a lengthy recipe for this very special carrot cake. It gave me joy to create this beautiful and delicious cake.

11

HEARTY FALL FEAST

CRAB-STUFFED CHICKEN
WITH HOLLANDAISE SAUCE

SALAD GREENS WITH
FRUIT AND BLUE CHEESE

CARAWAY PUFFS

BUTTER PECAN
PUMPKIN PIE

CRAB-STUFFED CHICKEN
WITH HOLLANDAISE SAUCE

- 8 BONELESS SKINLESS CHICKEN BREASTS
- SALT AND PEPPER TO TASTE
- ½ C CHOPPED ONION
- ½ C CHOPPED CELERY
- 3 T BUTTER
- 3 T WHITE WINE
- 1 (7-OZ) CAN CRAB MEAT, DRAINED
- ½ C HERB-SEASONED STUFFING MIX
- 2 T FLOUR
- ½ TSP PAPRIKA
- 2 T BUTTER, MELTED
- 1 C SHREDDED SWISS CHEESE

Recipe from St. Louis Jr. League cookbook, *Meet Us in the Kitchen*.

Preheat oven to 375°F.

Assemble Pound chicken breasts between 2 sheets of waxed paper to flatten. Season with salt and pepper. Sauté onion and celery in 3 tablespoons butter in a skillet until tender. Remove from heat. Add the wine, crab meat and stuffing mix and toss to mix well. Spoon the stuffing mixture onto each chicken breast. Fold in the sides and roll up; secure with wooden toothpicks. Mix the flour and paprika in a shallow dish, and dredge the chicken roll-ups in it. Arrange seam-side down in a glass baking dish. Drizzle with 2 tablespoons melted butter.

Bake uncovered for 40 minutes or until chicken is cooked through.

Serve Place the chicken on individual serving plates. Spoon the sauce over the chicken, adding additional stuffing if desired. Garnish with shredded cheese.

HOLLANDAISE SAUCE

- 4 EGG YOLKS
- 1 T FRESHLY SQUEEZED LEMON JUICE
- ½ C UNSALTED BUTTER, MELTED
- PINCH CAYENNE
- PINCH SALT

Vigorously whisk the egg yolks and lemon juice together in a stainless steel bowl until the mixture is thickened and doubled in volume. Place the bowl over a saucepan containing barely simmering water (or use a double boiler). The water should not touch the bottom of the bowl. Continue to whisk rapidly. Be careful not to let the eggs get too hot or they will scramble. Slowly drizzle in the melted butter and continue to whisk until the sauce is thickened and doubled in volume. Remove from heat, whisk in cayenne and salt. Cover and place in a warm spot until ready to use. If the sauce gets too thick, whisk in a few drops of warm water before serving.

SALAD GREENS WITH FRUIT AND BLUE CHEESE

SALAD
1 BUNCH RED LEAF LETTUCE, TORN INTO BITE-SIZED PIECES
1 BUNCH ROMAINE LETTUCE, TORN INTO BITE-SIZED PIECES
½ C EACH RED AND GREEN SEEDLESS GRAPES, HALVED
½ C WALNUT PIECES, TOASTED
1 GRANNY SMITH APPLE, DICED
2 OZ MAYTAG BLUE CHEESE, CRUMBLED

DRESSING
½ C SUGAR
⅓ C RED WINE VINEGAR
¾ C SALAD OIL
3 T GRATED ONION
1 TSP SALT
1 TSP DRY MUSTARD
2 TSP POPPY SEEDS

Place the greens, grapes, nuts, apple and cheese into a large salad bowl. Whisk dressing ingredients to emulsify. Pour a little of the salad dressing over the salad and toss to combine. Add more dressing to taste.

Serves 8-10.

CARAWAY PUFFS

- 1 PKG (¼ OZ) ACTIVE DRY YEAST
- ¼ C WARM WATER (110°F TO 115°F)
- 1 C WARM COTTAGE CHEESE (110°F TO 115°F) SMALL CURD
- 1 EGG
- 2 T SUGAR
- 1 T BUTTER OR MARGARINE, SOFTENED
- ¼ TSP BAKING POWDER
- 2 TSP CARAWAY SEEDS
- 1 TSP SALT
- ¼ TSP BAKING SODA
- 2-3 TSP GRATED ONION
- 1⅓ C SIFTED ALL-PURPOSE FLOUR
- 1 C SIFTED ALL-PURPOSE FLOUR

Preheat oven to 400°F.

In a mixing bowl, dissolve yeast in warm water. Add the cottage cheese, egg, sugar, butter, baking powder, caraway seeds, salt, baking soda, onion and 1⅓ cups flour; beat on low speed for 30 seconds. Beat on high for 3 minutes. Stir in the remaining flour (batter will be stiff). Do not knead. Cover and let rise in a warm place until doubled, about 45 minutes. Stir dough down. Spoon into greased muffin cups. Cover and let rise in a warm place until doubled, about 35 minutes. Bake 12-14 minutes or until golden brown.

Cool in pan for 1 minute. Serve immediately.

Yields 1 dozen.

BUTTER PECAN PUMPKIN PIE

1 9-INCH PIE SHELL, BAKED, COOLED

PIE
1 QT BUTTER PECAN ICE CREAM
1 C CANNED PUMPKIN
¾ C SUGAR
½ TSP SALT
¼ TSP EACH CINNAMON,
   GINGER, NUTMEG
1 C HEAVY CREAM, WHIPPED

SAUCE
½ C BROWN SUGAR
¼ C DARK CORN SYRUP
¼ C HOT WATER
1 TSP VANILLA

This pie is a breeze to make – if you start early locating butter pecan ice cream. It is a great dessert to make ahead and store in the freezer. With the easy sauce it becomes a glamorous finish for this hearty meal.

Pie Soften the ice cream and spread in the bottom of the baked pie shell. Freeze until hardened. Mix pumpkin, sugar, salt, cinnamon, ginger and nutmeg until smooth. Fold in the whipped cream. Spread atop the ice cream in the pie shell. Freeze until serving time.

Sauce Mix first three ingredients in a saucepan, bring to a boil, lower temperature and cook at a slow boil for 4 minutes. When cool, add vanilla. Sauce will thicken as it cools.

Remove pie from freezer 20-25 minutes before serving. Cut into wedges and drizzle sauce on top.

Becky Ritchey

I've always been involved with food. My college major was home economics. I cooked for the family, and then my husband was a bank executive, so I needed to learn entertaining. Making the Butter Pecan Pumpkin Pie is very satisfying because everyone seems to really enjoy it. It makes a great dinner-party ending.

12

IN THE TEX-MEX STYLE

CHEESE AND SHRIMP
STUFFED ROASTED
POBLANO CHILIES WITH
RED BELL PEPPER SAUCE

MEXICAN CHOPPED SALAD
WITH CITRUS VINAIGRETTE

SOUTHWESTERN
CORN BREAD PUDDING

CHEDDAR BUTTERMILK
CORN BREAD

SPANISH ALMOND FLAN

CHEESE AND SHRIMP STUFFED POBLANOS

8 LARGE POBLANO CHILIES, EACH ABOUT 3 OZ
8 OZ PEELED DEVEINED COOKED SHRIMP, COARSELY CHOPPED
⅔ C SOFT GOAT CHEESE (4 OZ) AT ROOM TEMPERATURE
½ C (PACKED) GRATED MONTEREY JACK CHEESE
¼ C CHOPPED RED PEPPER
2 T CHOPPED SHALLOT
2 T CHOPPED FRESH CILANTRO
2 T CHOPPED FRESH BASIL
1 RECIPE RED BELL PEPPER SAUCE
FRESH BASIL LEAVES FOR GARNISH

Char poblano chilies over gas flame or in a broiler until blackened on all sides. Enclose in paper bag for 10 minutes. Peel chilies. Using a small sharp knife, carefully slit chilies open along one side, leaving stems attached. Remove seeds.

Mix shrimp and next 6 ingredients in a medium bowl. Season to taste with salt and pepper. Fill chilies with the shrimp mixture, dividing equally. Pull up sides to enclose filling. Place stuffed chilies on a baking sheet. (Can be prepared one day ahead.)

Preheat oven to 350°F. Bake chilies uncovered until heated through and cheeses melt, about 15 minutes. Spoon 3 tablespoons Red Bell Pepper Sauce onto each of 8 plates. Place 1 stuffed chili on each. Garnish with basil leaves if desired.

Charring and peeling the peppers is an involved process and might be easier done a day ahead. It isn't hard and is well worth the effort.

Serves 8.

RED BELL PEPPER SAUCE

2 LARGE RED BELL PEPPERS
1 T OLIVE OIL
¼ C CHOPPED SHALLOTS
2 GARLIC CLOVES, MINCED
1 SERRANO OR JALAPEÑO CHILI, SEEDED AND MINCED
1 C LOW-SALT CHICKEN BROTH

Char bell peppers over a gas flame or in a broiler until blackened on all sides. Enclose in a paper bag 10 minutes. Peel, seed and coarsely chop bell peppers. Heat oil in a medium skillet over medium heat. Add the shallots, garlic and chili; sauté until the shallots are tender, about 5 minutes. Cool slightly. Transfer mixture to a blender; add bell peppers and chicken broth. Puree until smooth. Season sauce to taste with salt and pepper. (Can be made one day ahead. Rewarm before serving.)

Serves 8.

MEXICAN CHOPPED SALAD
WITH CITRUS VINAIGRETTE

VINAIGRETTE
- ½ TSP CUMIN
- ½ TSP CORIANDER
- DASH CAYENNE PEPPER
- 1 CLOVE OF GARLIC, MINCED
- 2 T FRESH ORANGE JUICE
- ¼ TSP ORANGE ZEST
- 2 T FRESH LIME JUICE
- ¼ TSP FINELY GRATED LIME ZEST
- ½ T AGAVE SYRUP OR HONEY
- 2½ T OLIVE OIL
- SEA SALT AND FRESHLY CRACKED PEPPER, TO TASTE

SALAD
- 1 C GRAPE TOMATOES, HALVED
- 2 GREEN ONIONS, CHOPPED
- 1 CAN BLACK BEANS, RINSED AND DRAINED
- 1 AVOCADO, DICED
- 1 SMALL ORANGE BELL PEPPER, DICED
- 1 C PRE-COOKED EDAMAME
- 1 C CORN, FROZEN (THAWED)
- 2 C ROMAINE LETTUCE, CHOPPED FINELY

GARNISHES
- COTIJA CHEESE, CRUMBLED (OR FETA CHEESE)
- 3 T FRESH CILANTRO, CHOPPED

Contest-winning recipe from Betterrecipes.com

Vinaigrette Combine the vinaigrette ingredients. Whisk until well combined. Set aside.

Salad Place the salad ingredients in a bowl; toss with vinaigrette to taste. When ready to serve, sprinkle with Cotija cheese and cilantro.

Cotija Cheese Cotija is a Hispanic-style cheese named after the town of Cotija in the Mexican state of Michoacán. This hard, crumbly Mexican cheese is made mainly from cow's milk. When the cheese is made, it is white, fresh and salty, bearing immense resemblance to feta cheese. However, with aging it becomes hard and crumbly like Parmigiano-Reggiano. Its similarity with Parmesan has earned it the nickname "Parmesan of Mexico." The aged version of Cotija is referred to as "anejo."

Serves 8-10.

Penny Moss

I love to make beautiful and delicious food! Cooking Club gives me a chance to make lemon meringue pie or rum cake because there is someone to share it with. This gorgeous salad is full of interesting shapes and bright colors. The vinaigrette is both tangy and sweet – perfect for this robust veggie salad.

SOUTHWESTERN CORN BREAD PUDDING

- 2 C FROZEN CORN KERNELS, THAWED AND DRAINED
- 2 C HOT MONTEREY PEPPER JACK CHEESE, COARSELY GRATED
- 1 MEDIUM BELL PEPPER, CHOPPED
- 1 ANAHEIM CHILI, SEEDED AND CHOPPED (AKA CALIFORNIA CHILI)
- ½ C GREEN ONIONS, CHOPPED
- 1¾ C BUTTERMILK
- 1 C CANNED ENCHILADA SAUCE
- 4 LARGE EGGS
- ½ TSP SALT

Butter a 9x3-inch glass baking dish or a 12-inch iron skillet. Cut corn bread (recipe below) into 1-inch cubes and place in large bowl. Stir corn kernels in a large dry skillet over medium heat, until excess moisture evaporates, about 3 minutes. Transfer to the bowl with the corn bread. Add cheese, bell pepper, chili and green onions. Whisk buttermilk, enchilada sauce, eggs and salt into a medium bowl to blend and then add to the corn bread mixture and toss gently to combine. Transfer mixture to the prepared pan. Cover and refrigerate at least one hour and up to one day. Preheat oven to 350°F. Bake corn bread pudding uncovered until slightly crisp and golden on top, about an hour. Let stand 10 minutes before serving. Cut into squares.

Serves 10-12.

CHEDDAR BUTTERMILK CORN BREAD

- 1 C ALL-PURPOSE FLOUR
- 1 C YELLOW CORN MEAL
- ¼ C SUGAR
- 2 TSP BAKING POWDER
- 1 TSP BAKING SODA
- 1 TSP SALT
- 1 C COARSELY GROUND EXTRA-SHARP CHEDDAR CHEESE
- 1 C BUTTERMILK
- 2 LARGE EGGS
- ¼ C UNSALTED BUTTER, MELTED AND COOLED SLIGHTLY

This cheesy corn bread is combined with the corn bread pudding recipe above, but it is very good on its own.

Preheat oven to 400°F. Butter an 8x8x2-inch metal pan. Whisk first 6 ingredients in a medium bowl to blend. Mix in cheese. In another medium bowl, whisk buttermilk, eggs and melted butter to blend. Add the buttermilk mixture to dry ingredients and stir just until incorporated; do not overmix. Transfer batter to prepared pan. Bake until golden on top and a tester inserted into the center comes out clean, about 22 minutes. Serve warm or at room temperature. (Can be made ahead, frozen, or stored for one day at room temperature.)

SPANISH ALMOND FLAN

½ C SUGAR
1 C SLIVERED ALMONDS, COARSELY GROUND
1 14-OZ CAN SWEETENED CONDENSED MILK
1 C CREAM
3 EGGS
3 EGG YOLKS
1 TSP VANILLA
WHIPPED CREAM

Preheat oven to 325°F. Sprinkle the sugar evenly in a wide skillet and place over medium heat. Caramelize the sugar by shaking the pan occasionally until the sugar is melted and has turned a light golden brown. A little stirring may be necessary when caramelizing the sugar over a gas burner. Pour into 9-inch cake pan. Allow to cool. The mixture may crack slightly.

In a blender or food processor, place the almonds. Blend on high for 3 seconds. Add sweetened condensed milk, cream, eggs and egg yolks, and vanilla. Blend for 10 seconds. Pour into the cake pan over the caramelized sugar. Set this pan into a larger pan containing ½-inch hot water. Bake 45 minutes (uncovered) or until set. Cool.

Place in refrigerator overnight. Do not remove until the next day. Loosen edges with a knife. Invert flan onto a chilled platter for presentation. Top each serving with whipped cream and toasted almonds. Can be made in 6 ramekins.

Serves 6-8.

Mary Ellen Randall

When my husband served in the army at Ft. Sill, Oklahoma, the Spanish liaison officer's wife gave me this unusual flan recipe. The almonds give it a texture and taste that is different from the traditional Spanish flan.

13

LADIES' BRIDGE LUNCHEON

CREAMY
AVOCADO-CUCUMBER
SOUP

FIESTA CHICKEN SALAD
WITH LIME CILANTRO
VINAIGRETTE

TINY ORANGE MUFFINS

WHITE CRÈME WITH
FRESH STRAWBERRIES

ALMOND COOKIES

CREAMY AVOCADO-CUCUMBER SOUP

3 LARGE CUCUMBERS – PEELED, SEEDED, AND COARSELY CHOPPED
1 LARGE AVOCADO, PEELED AND PITTED
2 T OLIVE OIL
2 LIMES, JUICED
1 LARGE CLOVE GARLIC
SALT AND GROUND BLACK PEPPER TO TASTE
½ C HEAVY CREAM
1 LARGE AVOCADO – PEELED, PITTED AND COARSELY CHOPPED
1 PINT CHERRY TOMATOES, HALVED

CONDIMENTS
FRESH CHIVES
CRISP CRUMBLED BACON
TOASTED ALMONDS

Place cucumbers, 1 avocado (peeled and pitted), olive oil, lime juice, garlic, salt and black pepper in a food processor. Add cream. Puree until smooth. Transfer to a serving bowl. Stir chopped avocado and tomatoes into soup. Chill overnight. Serve very cold, with condiments generously sprinkled on top.

Serves 6.

Jodie Louis

This is a very simple, easy, cold soup – perfect for hot summer afternoons. The tomatoes and avocado give it splashes of color. If you like, add a small jalapeño for some kick! It is beautiful served in a stemmed goblet, as we did, or a small bowl.

FIESTA CHICKEN SALAD
WITH LIME CILANTRO VINAIGRETTE

SALAD
- 3 C THINLY SLICED RED LEAF LETTUCE
- 3 C THINLY SLICED NAPA CABBAGE OR ROMAINE LETTUCE
- 1 C DICED COOKED CHICKEN BREAST
- 2 ROMA TOMATOES, SEEDED AND CHOPPED
- ½ RED BELL PEPPER, THINLY SLICED
- ½ YELLOW BELL PEPPER, THINLY SLICED
- ½ AVOCADO, PEELED AND SLICED
- ⅓ C CRUMBLED TORTILLA CHIPS
- ¼ C COOKED FRESH CORN KERNELS
- ¼ C PUMPKIN SEEDS, TOASTED
- ¼ C RED ONION, THINLY SLICED
- ½ C FETA CHEESE, CRUMBLED

VINAIGRETTE
- ½ C CHOPPED SHALLOTS
- ¼ C FRESH LIME JUICE
- ¼ C CHOPPED CILANTRO
- 1 T GARLIC, MINCED
- SALT AND FRESHLY GROUND PEPPER, TO TASTE
- ½ C VEGETABLE OIL

Salad Combine the salad ingredients, except the cheese, in a large bowl. Toss with enough vinaigrette to coat. Top with cheese.

Vinaigrette Whisk together the first five ingredients. Gradually add the vegetable oil, whisking until well blended.

Serves 6-8.

Barb Mohney

The Fiesta Chicken Salad is just my style. It is so easy to make, even an untrained cook like myself can't go wrong. I love the Mexican affinity of the salad. We like spending time in the Southwest, and would cheer having such a salad served to us. I was enticed into joining the Cooking Club because of family stories from my great-grandmother and grandmother, who were members in the past. Unfortunately, they didn't deliver to me a treasure trove of secret recipes, but there are some family treats that may have once been served at a long-ago TACC meeting. In any case, being in the club is great fun, and always a learning experience.

TINY ORANGE MUFFINS

MUFFINS
½ C BUTTER
1 C SUGAR
2 EGGS
1 TSP BAKING SODA
1 C BUTTERMILK
2 C ALL-PURPOSE FLOUR
GRATED ZEST OF 2 ORANGES
½ C GOLDEN RAISINS

TOPPING
JUICE OF 2 ORANGES
1 C BROWN SUGAR

Preheat oven to 400°F.

Muffins In large bowl, cream butter and sugar. Add eggs and beat until well mixed. Dissolve baking soda in buttermilk and add to mixture alternately with flour. Add orange zest and raisins. Fill well-buttered tiny muffin pans ¾ full, and bake 15 minutes. Remove immediately.

Topping In a small bowl, mix orange juice and brown sugar. Pour 1 teaspoon of the mixture on each warm muffin. Top with additional grated zest, if desired. Best when served warm.

Yields 4-5 dozen.

Warning: These little guys are going to smell and look so good you will want to eat the whole plate of them. They are sweet and soft and every bit as flavorful as they look, with the delicious orange glaze on top. They will brighten your day.

WHITE CRÈME WITH FRESH STRAWBERRIES

2 8-OZ CONTAINERS MASCARPONE CHEESE
½ C SUGAR
½ C MILK
STRAWBERRIES, QUANTITY AS DESIRED
SUGAR

Beat the mascarpone cheese, sugar and milk in electric mixer 5-7 minutes until thick. Chill for 1 hour. Cut strawberries in pieces and mix with sugar. Chill, then serve in small bowl with strawberries on top.

Serves 8.

ALMOND COOKIES

1 C BUTTER
1 C SUGAR
2 C FLOUR
½ TSP BAKING SODA
½ TSP SALT
1 TSP ALMOND EXTRACT
SLICED ALMONDS

Preheat oven to 350°F.

Cream the butter and sugar. Add the rest of the ingredients. Roll into 1-inch balls and roll them in sugar. Flatten with your thumb and put an almond slice into the depression. Bake for 12-15 minutes. Do not overbake.

Yields 5 dozen.

Pam Lester

I really enjoy all kinds of cooking, but my favorite recipes are the ones that allow natural flavors to be the featured element. The White Cream is like that. It is so simple to make, and yet it has a delicate elegance. The easy Almond Cookies are a perfect accompaniment. I learned the White Cream recipe and many others from a teacher in Tuscany who spoke a sort of broken English. She lives in a 400-year-old farmhouse. Much of the food she serves is grown in her vast garden.

14

CHRISTMAS LUNCHEON

ROASTED SALMON
WITH DILL, CAPERS
AND WASABI

✦

BEET, FARRO AND
WATERCRESS SALAD
WITH FIG VINAIGRETTE

✦

TRIPLE CHOCOLATE
MOUSSE CAKE

✦

SAVORY PINWHEELS

ROASTED SALMON WITH DILL, CAPERS AND WASABI

1 (3 LB) SALMON FILET
1 TSP KOSHER SALT
1 TSP FRESHLY GROUND BLACK PEPPER
¼ C FINELY GRATED FRESH WASABI (PASTE) (OR HORSERADISH)
2 T CHOPPED FRESH FLAT-LEAF PARSLEY
2 T FINELY CHOPPED SHALLOTS
3 T CAPERS, DRAINED AND CHOPPED
3 T OLIVE OIL

DILL SAUCE
¼ C HEAVY WHIPPING CREAM
1½ TSP BUTTERMILK
1 TSP WHITE WINE VINEGAR
2 T CHOPPED FRESH DILL
⅛ TSP KOSHER SALT
⅛ TSP FRESHLY GROUND BLACK PEPPER

Salmon Combine ingredients and spread evenly over salmon. Cover and refrigerate overnight.

Dill Sauce Combine cream, buttermilk and vinegar in a small bowl. Cover with plastic wrap and let stand at room temperature for 8 hours. Stir in dill, ⅛ teaspoon salt and ⅛ teaspoon pepper. Cover and refrigerate overnight.

Preheat oven to 450°F. Place fish, skin-side down on a parchment-lined baking sheet. Bake 13 minutes. Remove from oven. Preheat broiler to high and broil 5 minutes or until desired doneness. Cut into 8 portions. Top fish with dill sauce.

Serves 8.

Mary Schurman

I seem to have earned the title of "Salmon Lady" – although only my best friends get to call me that. It comes from my love of fish, and especially salmon. I grew up in the fishing culture around Lake Michigan, where grilling on the beach is an everyday event.

BEET, FARRO AND WATERCRESS SALAD
WITH FIG VINAIGRETTE

SALAD
- 1 LB BEETS, GOLDEN OR RED, SCRUBBED
- 6 T EXTRA-VIRGIN OLIVE OIL, DIVIDED
- ½ C UNCOOKED FARRO
- 2 C VERY THINLY SLICED FENNEL BULB
- 1½ C CUBED ZUCCHINI (½-INCH)
- 3 OZ WATERCRESS
- ½ C CHOPPED UNSALTED ROASTED ALMONDS

DRESSING
- ⅓ C RED WINE VINEGAR
- ¼ C FINELY CHOPPED DRIED FIGS
- 1 T CHOPPED FRESH THYME
- ¾ TSP KOSHER SALT
- ½ TSP FRESHLY GROUND BLACK PEPPER

Salad Preheat oven to 400°F. Leave root and 1-inch stem on beets. Rub beets with 1 tablespoon oil, wrap tightly in foil and roast beets at 400°F for 1½ hours or until very tender. Cool 15 minutes. Trim off beet roots; rub off skins, discard. Cut beets into wedges. Cook farro according to package directions: drain. Rinse under cold water, drain well. Spread farro on paper towels to dry out slightly. Add beet wedges, farro, fennel, zucchini and watercress to salad bowl.

Dressing Place vinegar and figs in a small saucepan. Cover and cook gently for 10 minutes over medium heat. Remove from heat; cool completely. Place vinegar mixture, thyme, salt and pepper in a large bowl; gradually add remaining 5 tablespoons of oil, stirring constantly with a whisk.

Add dressing to salad, and toss to coat. Sprinkle with almonds.

This is a hearty dish that could serve as a main dish for a vegetarian dinner. Farro is a grain that adds a somewhat crunchy texture and absorbs the wonderful flavors of the salad. The fig dressing fills the room with a sweet aroma while cooking and does not disappoint in tasting.

TRIPLE CHOCOLATE MOUSSE CAKE

CAKE LAYER
10 OZ HIGH-QUALITY SEMISWEET CHOCOLATE (CHOPPED)
4 LARGE EGGS (ROOM TEMPERATURE) SEPARATED
⅓ C SUGAR
¼ TSP SALT
1 TSP VANILLA EXTRACT
½ C BUTTER (ROOM TEMPERATURE)

CHOCOLATE MOUSSE LAYER
10 OZ HIGH-QUALITY SEMISWEET CHOCOLATE (CHOPPED)
1½ C HEAVY WHIPPING CREAM, DIVIDED
1 TSP UNFLAVORED GELATIN
2 T COOL WATER

WHITE CHOCOLATE MOUSSE LAYER
7 OZ HIGH-QUALITY WHITE CHOCOLATE (CHOPPED)
1½ C HEAVY WHIPPING CREAM
1 TSP UNFLAVORED GELATIN
2 T COOL WATER

This mousse cake is really worth the couple of days that it takes to make it. Each layer needs time to cool and set. The finished cake is beautiful and delicious!

Cake Preheat oven to 350°F. Lightly grease 9- or 10-inch spring form pan and line the bottom with parchment paper. The cake should be baked in a water bath so the edges don't dry out. Wrap the pan in two layers of aluminum foil and place it in a larger pan with about 1 inch of hot water.

Melt chocolate on low heat over a double boiler or in the microwave. Place egg whites in a large bowl with about a third of the sugar and beat on low speed until the mixture begins to look fluffy. Then add the remaining sugar, salt and vanilla. Continue beating until all sugar is dissolved and meringue looks shiny (nearly soft peak stage). Whisk softened butter into the melted chocolate until combined, then whisk in the egg yolks. Add half the meringue mixture into the chocolate and whisk gently, then fold the remaining meringue into the chocolate mixture. Remember to mix well the chocolate at the bottom of the bowl.

Pour batter into the prepared pan and bake for 26-28 minutes – until a toothpick inserted into the center comes out clean. When you remove the cake from the oven, first let it cool to room temperature, and then refrigerate for 1 hour. It will lose some volume. Remove from fridge and run a knife around the edge of the pan. Remove the ring from the pan and invert the cake onto a serving plate. Remove the pan bottom and parchment paper. Replace the ring around the cake to use as a mold for the mousse layers.

Chocolate Mousse Place chocolate in a heat-proof bowl. In a small dish soften 1 teaspoon unflavored gelatin in 2 tablespoons cool water; set aside for 5 minutes. Bring the ½ cup heavy cream to a boil, stir in the gelatin, and pour it over the chopped chocolate, stirring gently until the chocolate is completely melted. Whip the remaining 1 cup of whipping cream until soft peaks form (do not over whip). Chocolate mixture must be free of lumps and the temperature should be about 80°F. (Too-cool chocolate may set up; too hot and the cream will melt.) Add about half of the whipped cream to the chocolate and whisk gently until combined. Then fold in the remaining whipped cream, making sure to incorporate chocolate at the bottom of the bowl. Spread the mousse over the top of the cooled cake in the ring and smooth it with a spatula. Refrigerate at least an hour.

White Chocolate Mousse Repeat directions for chocolate mousse layer, using white chocolate ingredients. Be careful not to overheat the white chocolate while melting or it will separate. Spread the white chocolate mousse over the top of the chocolate mousse and refrigerate for at least 4-5 hours (or overnight).

Before serving, run a knife around the edge, and lift off the spring-form ring. Garnish the cake with chocolate curls or shavings if desired. Store in the fridge. Cake can be frozen for several weeks.

CHOCOLATE LEAVES
(OPTIONAL)

YIELD ABOUT 40 LEAVES
8 OZ BITTERSWEET (NOT UNSWEETENED) OR SEMISWEET CHOCOLATE, CHOPPED
40 ASSORTED SIZES OF LEAVES, WIPED CLEAN (LEMON LEAVES HAVE NICE VEINS)

Recipe from *Bon Appétit*, December 2003.

Line large baking sheet with foil. Melt chocolate in top of double boiler over simmering water, stirring until smooth and instant-read thermometer inserted into chocolate registers 115°F. Using a small artist brush, spread chocolate over veined side (underside) of leaves, coating thickly and completely, re-warming chocolate if necessary. Leaving chocolate side up, chill leaves until firm, about 45 minutes. Coat leaves a second time and chill again. Starting at stem end, carefully pull back green leaf, releasing chocolate leaf; return leaves to same baking sheet. (Can be made 2 days ahead. Cover and keep chilled.)

Jane Kuhlman

Entertaining family and friends is very important to me. I love to cook, and I especially enjoy making cookies to share.

SAVORY PINWHEELS

1 SHEET PUFF PASTRY
1 EGG WHITE
1 T GRATED LEMON ZEST
1½ TSP FRESH THYME, FINELY CHOPPED
1 TSP COARSE SEA SALT

Preheat oven to 400°F. Thaw one sheet of puff pastry dough according to package directions, and place on a lightly floured work surface. Brush with beaten egg white, then sprinkle with zest, thyme and salt. Starting at short side, roll up like a jelly roll. Cut into 20 ½-inch slices. Bake 15-16 minutes or until lightly browned.

Makes 20.

15

ITALIAN PRANZO

NORTHERN ITALIAN
LASAGNA TORTE

QUICK
ITALIAN SALAD

PARMESAN TOAST

TORTA DI MELE
(ITALIAN APPLE CAKE)
WITH CARAMEL SAUCE

NORTHERN ITALIAN LASAGNA TORTE

MEAT SAUCE
3 T OLIVE OIL
2 RIBS CELERY, CHOPPED
1 CARROT, CHOPPED
1 SMALL ONION, CHOPPED
¼ C CHOPPED PARSLEY
2 CLOVES GARLIC, MINCED
½ LB ITALIAN SAUSAGE, CASING REMOVED
28-OZ CAN ITALIAN TOMATOES, CUT UP
6-OZ CAN TOMATO PASTE
⅓ C WHITE WINE
1 TSP BASIL
½ TSP EACH MARJORAM AND OREGANO
SALT AND FRESHLY GROUND BLACK PEPPER TO TASTE

WHITE SAUCE
3 T BUTTER
¼ C FLOUR
2½ C MILK
½ C GRATED PARMESAN CHEESE
½ TSP SALT
½ TSP CAYENNE PEPPER

PASTA
12 OZ CURLY-EDGED LASAGNA NOODLES, COOKED

3 C SHREDDED MOZZARELLA CHEESE

Meat sauce Heat oil in saucepan. Sauté celery, onion, carrot, parsley and garlic until softened. Add sausage, cook until lightly browned. Stir in tomatoes, tomato paste, wine and seasonings. Bring to a boil. Simmer uncovered 20 minutes or until slightly thickened, stirring occasionally.

White sauce Melt butter in saucepan. Stir in flour, cooking until bubbly. Add milk; cook, stirring constantly, until sauce boils and thickens. Remove from heat. Stir in Parmesan cheese. Season with salt and pepper. Cook noodles only until soft and pliable; drain.

Heat oven to 350°F. Grease 9-inch spring form pan. Assemble as follows:

1st layer Place one-fourth noodles, overlapping to cover bottom of pan, curving so that curly edges are around the rim of the pan. Spread half of white sauce and 1 cup mozzarella over noodles.

2nd layer Place one-fourth noodles and half of meat sauce over first layer.

3rd layer Place one-fourth noodles, remaining white sauce and 1 cup mozzarella over second layer.

4th layer Top with remaining noodles, remaining meat sauce and sprinkle remaining mozzarella around the edge.

Place pan on baking sheet; bake 30 minutes or until bubbly and heated through. Let stand 10 minutes. Carefully remove rim from pan, let stand another 10 minutes. Cut into wedges and serve. Can be made a day in advance, covered with plastic and refrigerated. Bake it the day you serve it, adding 10-15 minutes in oven if it is cold.

Marla Chandler

I grew up in a large, close-knit family, and learned to cook from my mother and grandmother. Good meals were an important part of everyday life. My menus today feature everything from healthy mid-American comfort food to Southwest, Asian, French and Italian-inspired dishes.

QUICK ITALIAN SALAD

SALAD
1 HEAD ICEBERG LETTUCE OR
  BOSTON BIBB LETTUCE
6 WHOLE PEPPERONCINI
½ C WHOLE BLACK OLIVES
½ C WHOLE RED CHERRY TOMATOES
½ SMALL RED ONION
⅓ C GRATED PARMESAN CHEESE

SALAD DRESSING
½ C OLIVE OIL
¼ C MAYONNAISE
¼ C GRATED PARMESAN CHEESE
¼ C MINCED FRESH PARSLEY
1 T SUGAR
1 T VINEGAR
2 TSP BLACK PEPPER
1 TSP SALT
¼ TSP RED PEPPER FLAKES
1 CLOVE GARLIC, PRESSED
JUICE OF ONE LEMON

Salad Roughly chop or tear lettuce and put into a large bowl. Toss with the dressing. Top the salad with the pepperoncini, banana peppers or preserved peppers. Slice onion thinly in circles and add with olives and tomatoes. Sprinkle with Parmesan at the end.

Dressing Puree the ingredients in a blender. This dressing is almost like a pesto – very tasty on many salads, and also as a dip.

Serves 6-8.

PARMESAN TOAST

½ LB DAY-OLD COUNTRY-STYLE BREAD
EXTRA VIRGIN OLIVE OIL
½ C FRESHLY GRATED
  PARMESAN CHEESE

Preheat oven to 350°F. Slice bread ¼ inch thick. Brush one side of bread with olive oil. Dust the oiled side with the Parmesan. Arrange on a baking sheet and bake until brown and crisp, 15-20 minutes. Serve warm or at room temperature.

Baguette slices are very attractive cut on the diagonal.

TORTA DI MELE (ITALIAN APPLE CAKE) WITH CARAMEL SAUCE

CAKE
- ¾ C BUTTER, SOFTENED
- 2 C SUGAR
- 2 EGGS
- 2 C ALL-PURPOSE FLOUR
- 2 TSP GROUND CINNAMON
- 2 TSP BAKING SODA
- ½ TSP GROUND NUTMEG
- ½ TSP SALT
- 4 C PEELED, FINELY CHOPPED APPLES (GRANNY SMITH, MACINTOSH OR JONATHAN)
- 1 TSP VANILLA EXTRACT

CARAMEL SAUCE
- ¾ C BUTTER
- ¾ C SUGAR
- ¾ C PACKED BROWN SUGAR
- ¾ C HEAVY CREAM
- 1½ TSP VANILLA

Preheat oven to 350°F. Grease a 13x9-inch cake pan.

Cake Cream butter and sugar in a large bowl. Beat in eggs one at a time. Whisk dry ingredients together and add to egg mixture alternately with apples. Stir in vanilla. Pour into prepared pan and bake for 40-45 minutes or until cake tests done with a toothpick. Cool in pan for 5 minutes before cutting into squares. Serve warm.

Sauce Combine all ingredients in a saucepan. Bring to a boil over medium heat, stirring constantly. Immediately remove from heat and spoon over individual servings of warm cake.

Serves 12.

Think of eating a caramel apple without getting caramel on your chin. This dessert is more apple than cake, with apples and cinnamon folded into a moist spice cake. The cake is delicious on its own, but the Caramel Sauce puts it over the top in flavor.

16

A FAMILY AFFAIR

ROMAINE, BEET AND
GOAT CHEESE SALAD

SAUSAGE CORN CHOWDER

NO-KNEAD DUTCH-OVEN
CRUSTY BREAD

MOOSELIPS
PUMPKIN CHEESECAKE

ROMAINE, BEET AND GOAT CHEESE SALAD

RASPBERRY DRESSING
½ C RASPBERRY BALSAMIC VINEGAR
1 T FRESH LEMON JUICE
1 TSP WATER
½ TSP SALT
½ TSP PIERRE POIVRE SPICE OR
　BLACK PEPPER
1 C OLIVE OIL

SALAD
4 C SMALL BEETS
2 HEARTS OF ROMAINE
4 C ARUGULA OR BOSTON LETTUCE
½ APPLE
1 TSP FRESH LEMON JUICE
SALT AND FRESHLY GROUND PEPPER
½ C RASPBERRY DRESSING
4 OZ GORGONZOLA, CUT INTO
　16 PIECES
2 OZ CHILLED GOAT CHEESE,
　CRUMBLED
¼ C PISTACHIOS, TOASTED

Dressing Combine ingredients except oil. Slowly pour in oil while whisking. Reserve.

Salad Cut the stems off the beets and steam for 15-20 minutes. Cool, then peel and cut into halves or quarters, depending on size.

Preheat broiler. Cut stems off romaine hearts, discard outer leaves and submerge in cold water to clean. Drain and place on towel to dry; reserve. Slice the apple thinly, and reserve in water with lemon juice. Place the goat cheese under the broiler until golden, then cut into 8 pieces. Place the romaine hearts and beets in a large bowl and season with salt, pepper and raspberry dressing. Divide among plates and add the apple, cheeses and toasted pistachios.

Serves 8.

Did You Say You Don't Like Beets?

Well, then you haven't tried this salad. Maybe you remember canned beets from your childhood. And maybe you've never had beets prepared really well. Roasting or steaming produces a superior flavor, color and texture. Combining them with something sweet, in this case, sweet raspberry dressing, brings out their sweetness and makes them tasty. And don't forget, beets are low in calories and contain vitamins A, B and C, beta-carotene, folic acid and many minerals, such as potassium and iron.

SAUSAGE CORN CHOWDER

CHOWDER
- ½ LB PORK SAUSAGE, (OPTIONAL – ROLLED INTO SMALL MEATBALLS)
- ½ C CHOPPED ONION
- ½ C CHOPPED GREEN BELL PEPPER (OR POBLANO PEPPER)
- 1 GARLIC CLOVE, MINCED
- ¼ C ALL-PURPOSE FLOUR
- 1 14-OZ CAN CHICKEN BROTH
- ½ C WHOLE MILK
- ½ C HEAVY CREAM
- ¾ TSP SALT
- ¾ TSP GROUND CUMIN (OR TOAST 1 WHOLE CUMIN, THEN GRIND IT)
- ¾ TSP FRESH GROUND PEPPER
- 2 C FROZEN CORN KERNELS
- 1 15-OZ CAN CREAM STYLE CORN
- ¼ C DICED RED BELL PEPPER
- 2-4 T CHOPPED FRESH CILANTRO
- 1 C SHREDDED MONTEREY JACK CHEESE (OPTIONAL)

GARNISH
- SHREDDED CHEDDAR CHEESE OR MEXICAN-STYLE BLENDED CHEESE
- CHOPPED FRESH PARSLEY OR CHOPPED FRESH CHIVES

Brown sausage, onion, green bell pepper and garlic in large heavy pan. Stir and break up sausage and cook until sausage is browned. If you use small meatballs, cook at low temperature until cooked through. Add flour and cook, stirring constantly about 1 minute. Stir in chicken broth, milk, cream, salt, cumin and pepper and continue to cook and stir over medium heat until mixture comes to a boil.

Stir in frozen corn, cream corn and red bell pepper. Cook over medium heat, stirring frequently, 10 to 20 minutes or until thoroughly heated and thickened. Stir in cilantro and 1 cup shredded cheese, if using. Garnish with a sprinkling of cheese and chopped fresh parsley. This soup freezes nicely.

Down-home and hearty, this tummy-warming chowder is both fresh and classic. It goes together quickly, serves a crowd, and tastes every bit as good the next day, and the next.

NO-KNEAD DUTCH-OVEN CRUSTY BREAD

3 C ALL-PURPOSE FLOUR
1¾ TSP SALT
½ TSP ACTIVE DRY YEAST
1½ C WATER – ROOM TEMPERATURE

NOTE: YOU WILL NEED A 3½-QT CAST IRON POT WITH A LID

In a big bowl mix the flour, salt and yeast together. Pour water into the bowl and, using a spatula or wooden spoon, mix until well incorporated. Cover the bowl with plastic wrap and let sit on the counter 12-18 hours.

Preheat oven to 450°F. Place your cast iron pot into the oven as it warms, and heat it to 450°F. Remove the pot from the oven and remove the lid. Sprinkle some flour or cornmeal on the bottom of the pot to prevent sticking. Flour your hands really well, and sprinkle a bit of flour over the dough. With floured hands, gently remove the dough from the bowl and roughly shape it into a ball. Drop the ball of dough into the pot, replace the lid and put the pot back in the oven. Bake 30 minutes with the lid on. Then, remove lid and bake an additional 20 minutes until dark golden brown. (You might want to slightly reduce the temperature for baking without the lid.) Remove the bread from the pot; it should fall out easily. Let cool completely before slicing and serving.

Yields 1½-lb. loaf.

This recipe, published by The New York Times, has become very popular. It comes from Jim Lahey, owner of Sullivan Street Bakery. It requires no kneading, but it takes time, although mostly it involves waiting.

MOOSELIPS PUMPKIN CHEESECAKE
WITH A CARAMEL SWIRL

CRUST
1 C FINE GRAHAM CRACKER CRUMBS
   (9 CRACKERS)
½ C FINE GINGERSNAP COOKIE CRUMBS
   (10 GINGERSNAP COOKIES)
¼ C FINELY CHOPPED WALNUTS
2 T GRANULATED SUGAR
¼ TSP GROUND GINGER
½ C BUTTER, MELTED

FILLING
3 8-OZ PACKAGES CREAM CHEESE,
   SOFTENED
¾ C GRANULATED SUGAR
½ C PACKED BROWN SUGAR
2 T CORNSTARCH
1 TSP GROUND CINNAMON
1 TSP VANILLA
½ TSP GROUND NUTMEG OR ALLSPICE
1 15-OZ CAN PUMPKIN
1 5-OZ CAN (2/3 C) EVAPORATED
   MILK
2 EGGS, LIGHTLY BEATEN

TOPPING
1 16-OZ CARTON DAIRY SOUR CREAM
⅓ C GRANULATED SUGAR
1 TSP VANILLA
2 T CARAMEL ICE CREAM TOPPING
CHOCOLATE CURLS OR CHOCOLATE
   LEAVES (OPTIONAL)

This recipe comes from Mooselips Java Joint in Seeley, Wisconsin.

Crust Preheat oven to 375°F. Be sure your ingredients are at room temperature. In a medium bowl, combine the first 5 ingredients. Stir in melted butter. Press crumb mixture onto the bottom and 2 inches up the sides of a 10-inch spring form pan. Bake for 5 minutes (do not allow crust to brown). Set aside.

Filling In a large mixing bowl, beat cream cheese, the ¾ cup granulated sugar, brown sugar, cornstarch, cinnamon, the 1 teaspoon vanilla and nutmeg with an electric mixer until combined. Beat in pumpkin and milk until smooth. Stir in eggs. Pour filling into crust-lined pan. Place spring form pan in a shallow baking pan to prevent spills in oven. Bake for 55 to 60 minutes or until a 2½-inch area around the outside edge appears set when gently shaken.

Topping In a small bowl, combine sour cream, the ⅓ cup granulated sugar and the 1 teaspoon vanilla. Spread evenly over the top of hot cheesecake. Drizzle the caramel topping over the sour cream mixture; with the tip of a knife, carefully swirl the caramel topping across the cake. Return cheesecake to the oven. Bake for 5 minutes more. Cool in pan on a wire rack for 15 minutes. Using a sharp knife, loosen the crust from sides of the pan; cool for 30 minutes more. Remove the sides of the pan; cool cheesecake completely on rack. Cover and chill for at least 4 hours before serving. If you like, serve with chocolate curls or leaves.

Serves 14-16.

17

FEASTING WITH FLAIR

AUTUMN CHICKEN AND
PHYLLO CRUST POT PIES

FESTIVE FRESH
FRUIT SALAD
WITH ORANGE
AMARETTO SAUCE

BROWNIE-BOTTOM
CRÈME BRULÈ

AUTUMN CHICKEN AND PHYLLO CRUST POT PIES

- 1-2 C APPLE CIDER
- 3 T BUTTER
- 1 LB BONELESS SKINLESS CHICKEN TENDERS, BREAST OR THIGHS
- 2 T OLIVE OIL
- 1 SMALL SWEET ONION, CHOPPED
- SALT AND PEPPER TO TASTE
- 2 CLOVES GARLIC
- 1 C BUTTERNUT SQUASH, PEELED AND CUBED
- 2 C BUTTON MUSHROOMS, CHOPPED
- 6 LEAVES FRESH SAGE, CHOPPED
- 1 T FRESH THYME, CHOPPED
- 6 T BUTTER
- ⅓ C FLOUR
- 1½ C CHICKEN BROTH OR USE APPLE CIDER
- 2 C MILK
- PINCH OF CAYENNE PEPPER
- 1 C FROZEN GREEN PEAS
- 18 SHEETS PHYLLO DOUGH
- MELTED BUTTER OR OLIVE OIL FOR BRUSHING
- ROASTED PUMPKIN OR BUTTERNUT SQUASH SEEDS, OPTIONAL

Add the apple cider, butter and chicken to a large pot and set over high heat, covered. Bring to a boil and then reduce the heat to a simmer. Simmer 20 minutes or until the chicken is cooked through. Remove the chicken from the cider and allow to cool. Shred the chicken with two forks or your hands.

Meanwhile, add the olive oil to a large skillet and set over medium heat. Once hot, add the onion and cook until softened and slightly caramelized, about 5 minutes, seasoning with salt and pepper. Add the garlic, butternut squash and mushrooms. Continue to cook until the squash is fork tender, about 10 minutes. Stir in the sage and thyme. Add the remaining 6 tablespoons butter. Once the butter has melted add the flour and cook, stirring to incorporate for a minute. Slowly pour in the chicken broth, milk and a pinch of cayenne. Bring the sauce to a low boil and then reduce the heat and stir in the peas. Simmer for 5 minutes or until the sauce has thickened. Remove from the heat. Stir in the shredded chicken. Taste and season with more salt and pepper if needed.

Preheat the oven to 375°F.

Lightly grease six 8-ounce ramekins with butter or cooking spray. Divide the chicken mixture evenly among the ramekins. Lay three pieces of phyllo dough flat on your counter. Liberally brush the top sheet with melted butter and squish the sheets together to fit over the top of your ramekin. Repeat with the remaining dough. Place the pot pies on a baking sheet and bake for 30 minutes or until the phyllo dough is golden and the filling is hot. Serve with fresh thyme and toasted pumpkin/butternut squash seeds if desired.

Makes 6 pot pies.

FESTIVE FRESH FRUIT SALAD

- 4 RIPE MANGOES
- 4 MEDIUM PEARS – RIPE
- 2 C SEEDLESS GREEN GRAPES
- 2 C SEEDLESS RED GRAPES
- 4 KIWI FRUIT
- 1 C STRAWBERRIES
- 2 BANANAS

Salad Peel, core and section mangoes. Core and slice pears. In a large bowl, combine the mangoes, pears and grapes. Pour chilled almond sauce over. Cover and refrigerate until well chilled, stirring occasionally. Peel and slice kiwi fruit, stem strawberries, cutting in half. Slice banana into thick slices. Gently stir into fruit mixture.

Serves 10-12.

A celebration of fruit in all shapes and colors and textures! The cool, silky almond sauce heightens the sophistication of this delightfully unique salad.

ORANGE AMARETTO SAUCE

- 1¼ C SUGAR
- 3 T FRESH LEMON JUICE
- ¼ TSP SALT
- 1 C WATER
- ¼ C AMARETTO LIQUEUR
- 2 T GRAND MARNIER OR TRIPLE SEC LIQUEUR

Sauce This sauce is so delicious and refreshing you might want to make a double batch. Poured over a plain banana or pear it would be a special treat.

In a 2-quart pan over medium heat, combine sugar, lemon juice, salt and water and cook for 5-10 minutes, or until mixture forms a light syrup. Stir in liqueurs and refrigerate until syrup is cool.

BROWNIE-BOTTOM CRÈME BRULÈ

BROWNIES
4 4½ OZ BITTERSWEET OR
    SEMI-SWEET CHOCOLATE
¼ C (½ STICK) UNSALTED BUTTER
½ C SUGAR
½ TSP VANILLA EXTRACT
¼ TSP SALT
1 LARGE EGG
¼ C FLOUR
¾ C CHOPPED PECANS

CUSTARD
3 C WHIPPING CREAM
½ VANILLA BEAN,
    SPLIT LENGTHWISE
6 LARGE EGG YOLKS
6 TSP SUGAR

FINISH
8 T SUGAR

Brownies Preheat oven to 350°F. Butter an 8x8-inch baking pan. Melt the chocolate and butter in a small saucepan over low heat. Stir until smooth and transfer to a large bowl. Cool for 10 minutes. Whisk the sugar, vanilla and salt into the chocolate mixture. Whisk in the egg. Add the flour and stir just until blended. Fold in the pecans. Smooth the top. Bake at 20 minutes or until set and pulling away from edges of pan. Cool on wire rack. Cut into 9 squares, or use round cutter to make circles.

Custard Pour the cream into a medium saucepan. Scrape the seeds from the vanilla bean into the cream and add the bean. Bring to a simmer and remove from heat. Discard the vanilla bean. Whisk the egg yolks and 6 tablespoons of sugar in a large bowl. Whisk a small amount of the hot mixture into the egg yolks; then whisk egg yolks into the hot mixture. Cook over medium-low heat for 2 minutes or until the mixture coats the spoon, stirring constantly. Do not boil. Pour through a fine strainer into a bowl.

Assemble Press one brownie square or circle into the bottom of each of eight ¾-cup ramekins; there will be one brownie left over. Pour the custard into the ramekins. Arrange in a large baking pan. Add enough hot water to the pan to come halfway up the cups. Cover the pan loosely with foil. Bake at 325°F for 45 minutes or until the custard is softly set. Remove the custards to a wire rack to cool. Chill for 3 hours or longer.

Finish Arrange the custards on a heavy baking sheet. Sprinkle 1 teaspoon of sugar on top of each custard. Broil for 2 minutes or until golden brown, watching carefully to avoid burning. Or use kitchen torch to brown the sugar tops. Serve immediately.

Note This brownie recipe is especially suited for the brulè recipe. Don't be tempted to use a brownie mix.

Anne Allen

I grew up watching my mom cook, and she is truly a great cook. In our home, holidays were always over the top with fabulous food and decorations. I love making delicious desserts with special touches, and I always have interesting tablescapes in my home. For my daughter I created a Pinterest-style cookbook with photos of her cooking. She actually uses it when she cooks.

18

KANSAS DINNER

ROASTED PORK TENDERLOIN
WITH CALVADOS CREAM SAUCE

GARLIC PARMESAN
ROASTED POTATOES

FALL SALAD WITH
BALSAMIC ITALIAN DRESSING

MOLTEN CHOCOLATE CAKES
WITH GRANDMOTHER SAUCE

ROASTED PORK TENDERLOIN
WITH CALVADOS CREAM SAUCE

2 T KOSHER SALT
1 T PACKED DARK BROWN SUGAR
1 T FINELY CHOPPED FRESH THYME LEAVES
2 TSP FRESHLY GROUND BLACK PEPPER
1 (4½ LBS) BONELESS PORK TENDERLOIN
1 T OLIVE OIL

ROASTING
1½ LBS CIPOLLINI ONIONS
12 OZ UNSLICED PANCETTA
2 T PACKED DARK BROWN SUGAR
1 TSP FINELY CHOPPED FRESH THYME
FRESHLY GROUND BLACK PEPPER

SAUCE
UNSALTED BUTTER, AS NEEDED
3 T ALL-PURPOSE FLOUR
1 C APPLE CIDER OR APPLE JUICE
1 C CALVADOS
2 C CHICKEN BROTH OR STOCK
½ TSP KOSHER SALT (MORE AS NEEDED)
¼ C HEAVY CREAM
FRESHLY GROUND BLACK PEPPER

For the pork Combine the salt, sugar, thyme and pepper in a small bowl; set aside. Pat the pork dry with paper towels and place on a baking sheet or large dish. Using your hands, rub it all over with the oil, sprinkle with all of the thyme mixture, and rub until evenly coated. Cover with plastic wrap and refrigerate for at least 2 hours or up to 24 hours. Peel the onions and place them in a large bowl. Cut the pancetta into large dice and add it to the bowl. Add the sugar and thyme, season with pepper, and toss with your hands to combine; set aside.

For roasting Heat the oven to 450°F. Place a rack in the middle. Place the pork fat-side up in the middle of a roasting pan and roast for 30 minutes. Reduce the oven temperature to 350°F, scatter the onion-pancetta mixture around the pork in an even layer, and roast for 20 minutes, stirring once. Continue to roast until the onions are knife tender and an instant-read thermometer inserted into the center of the pork registers 145°F, about 10 to 20 minutes more. Transfer the pork to a large plate and loosely tent with aluminum foil. Using a slotted spoon, transfer the onion-pancetta mixture to a serving dish, cover with aluminum foil, and set aside while you make the sauce.

For the sauce Drain all but 3 tablespoons of drippings from the roasting pan adding butter if needed. Place the pan over medium heat. Sprinkle in the flour and scrape up any browned bits from the bottom of the pan. Cook, stirring constantly, until the raw taste of the flour is cooked out, about 2 to 3 minutes. Increase the heat to medium high. Whisk in the cider or juice and Calvados and cook, whisking occasionally, until the sauce simmers and thickens, about 5 to 6 minutes. Whisk in the broth or stock and measured salt and bring to a boil. Cook, stirring occasionally, until reduced to about 2¼ cups, about 5 minutes. Pour the mixture through a strainer into a medium saucepan. Discard the contents of the strainer. Place the saucepan over medium heat, whisk in the cream and any accumulated juices on the plate from the rested pork, and bring to a simmer. Taste and season with salt and pepper as needed. Transfer to a serving bowl. Cut the pork crosswise into ½-inch-thick slices. Serve with the onion-pancetta mixture and sauce.

Serves 6.

GARLIC PARMESAN ROASTED POTATOES

- 3 LBS RED POTATOES, HALVED
- 2 T OLIVE OIL
- 5 CLOVES GARLIC, MINCED
- 1 TSP FRESH THYME
- 1 TSP FRESH OREGANO
- 1 TSP FRESH BASIL
- ⅓ C FRESHLY GRATED PARMESAN
- KOSHER SALT AND FRESHLY GROUND BLACK PEPPER TO TASTE
- 2 T UNSALTED BUTTER
- 2 T CHOPPED FRESH PARSLEY LEAVES

Preheat oven to 400°F. Coat a baking sheet with nonstick spray or use Silpat liner. Place potatoes in a single layer on the baking sheet. Mix seasonings and cheese to combine and gently toss with potatoes. Bake for 25-30 minutes or until golden brown and crisp. Stir in butter until melted, about one minute. Serve immediately, garnished with parsley if desired.

FALL SALAD
WITH BALSAMIC ITALIAN DRESSING

GLAZED WALNUTS
2 C WALNUTS
¼ C SUGAR
2 T WATER

SALAD
10 OZ ARUGULA
2 HEADS HEARTS OF ROMAINE
1 RED ONION
1 RED BELL PEPPER
1 C RAISINS (YELLOW OPTIONAL)

DRESSING
1 PKG ITALIAN DRESSING
   (GOOD SEASONS BRAND)
2 T BALSAMIC VINEGAR
½ C VEGETABLE OIL
2 T WATER
¼ TSP CAYENNE PEPPER
1 TSP SUGAR

Glazed Walnuts Place walnuts, sugar and water in saucepan. Cook 4 minutes or until sugar lightly boils. Pour into a jelly roll pan and let cool.

Salad Rinse and chop lettuce. Peel and chop red onion. De-seed and dice red bell pepper and place all together in a serving bowl. Cover and chill. Just before serving, toss with raisins and walnuts.

Dressing Mix all ingredients together in a blender and chill before serving. When ready to serve, toss with Fall Salad.

This balsamic vinaigrette is great for the beautiful salad. Using a packet of Good Seasons seasoning mix is an easy way to combine perfect spices into a homemade dressing that zings with flavor.

Nancy Brammer

Club luncheons have always been lovely, but in recent years we have begun to apply even more creativity to menu choices, table settings and flower arrangements. The chocolate cupcakes in this menu are a true show stopper. Oohs and ahs fill the room when the molten interior flows out. It is such a satisfying response.

MOLTEN CHOCOLATE CAKES
WITH GRANDMOTHER SAUCE

GANACHE
¼ C HEAVY CREAM
2 OZ BITTERSWEET CHOCOLATE, CHOPPED INTO SMALL PIECES

CAKES
5 OZ BITTERSWEET CHOCOLATE, CHOPPED INTO SMALL PIECES
6 T UNSALTED BUTTER, PLUS MORE FOR RAMEKINS
DEMERARA OR RAW SUGAR FOR SPRINKLING
3 LARGE EGGS
⅓ C LIGHT BROWN SUGAR
1 TSP VANILLA EXTRACT
3 T ALL-PURPOSE FLOUR
½ TSP KOSHER SALT

GRANDMOTHER SAUCE
1 C WHIPPING CREAM
1 EGG
½ C SUGAR
2 T BUTTER, MELTED
½ TSP VANILLA EXTRACT

NOTE: THIS SAUCE CONTAINS RAW EGG. THERE ARE EGG SUBSTITUTES WHICH MAY BE USED, OR THE EGG MAY BE DELETED FROM THE RECIPE, WITH LESS RICHNESS.

A delicious treat made easy! This recipe by *Bon Appétit* adds a small morsel of ganache into the middle of the little cake. The whole cake is baked through, and the chocolate ganache oozes out.

Ganache Heat cream in small saucepan over medium heat until just beginning to simmer. Place 2 ounces chocolate in a small bowl; pour cream over. Stir until smooth. Chill ganache until firm, at least 1 hour.

Cakes Preheat oven to 425°F. Coat ramekins or custard cups with butter and sprinkle with Demerara sugar, tapping out excess. Combine 6 tablespoons butter and remaining 5 ounces chocolate in a medium heatproof bowl set over a large saucepan of barely simmering water (do not let water touch the bowl). Stir constantly until chocolate is melted (you can also do this step in the microwave). Using an electric mixer on medium-high speed, beat eggs and brown sugar in large bowl until light and tripled in volume, about 4 minutes. Beat in vanilla. Gently fold melted chocolate into egg mixture until incorporated. Fold in flour and salt until smooth. Divide half of batter among prepared ramekins (about ⅓ cup each.) Place 1 mounded tablespoon ganache in the center of each partially filled ramekin. Divide remaining batter among ramekins. Bake until tops are firm but cakes wobble slightly when jiggled, 13-15 minutes. Let cool 30 seconds before inverting onto small plates. Serve immediately with Grandmother Sauce.

Do Ahead: Ganache may be made 1 week ahead. Tightly wrap and keep chilled. Cakes can be assembled 1 week ahead, wrapped in plastic and frozen. Let sit at room temperature 1 hour before baking.

Grandmother Sauce Whip the cream in a large mixing bowl. In a medium bowl, beat the egg with an electric mixer until thick and lemony colored. Gradually add sugar, beating until thickened, about 2-3 minutes. Stir in the butter and vanilla. Gently fold in the whipped cream. Chill at least 1-3 hours so the sugar dissolves.

Serves 4.

19

EASY ELEGANCE

SPANAKOPITA
GREEK SPINACH PIE

ASPARAGUS SALAD

MARITA'S CRANBERRY ORANGE
BREAD PUDDING
WITH GRAND MARNIER SAUCE

SPANAKOPITA GREEK SPINACH PIE

2 T OLIVE OIL
3 C YELLOW ONION, CHOPPED
1 BUNCH GREEN ONIONS, CHOPPED
2 TSP KOSHER SALT
1⅓ TSP FRESHLY GROUND PEPPER
3 PKG FROZEN CHOPPED SPINACH, DEFROSTED
6 EXTRA-LARGE EGGS, BEATEN
2 TSP NUTMEG
½ C GRATED PARMESAN CHEESE
3 T PLAIN DRY BREAD CRUMBS
½ LB GOOD FETA, CUT INTO ½-INCH CUBES
½ C PINE NUTS
¼ C SALTED BUTTER, MELTED OR BUTTER-FLAVORED SPRAY
6 SHEETS PHYLLO DOUGH, DEFROSTED

Preheat oven to 375°F.

In a medium sauté pan on medium heat, sauté the onions with the olive oil until they are translucent and slightly browned, 10-15 minutes. Add the salt and pepper and allow to cool slightly. Wrap the spinach in a clean towel and squeeze out as much of the liquid as possible.

Put the spinach into a bowl and then gently add the onions, eggs, nutmeg, Parmesan cheese, bread crumbs, feta and pine nuts.

Butter an ovenproof, nonstick 8-inch sauté pan or a 9-inch glass pie pan. Line it with 6 stacked sheets of phyllo dough, brushing each with melted butter or spraying with butter spray. Let the edges of the sheets hang over the side. Pour the spinach mixture into the middle of the phyllo and neatly fold the edges up and over the top to seal in the filling. Brush the top well with butter or spray. Bake for one hour until the top is golden brown and the filling is set. Remove from the oven and allow to cool completely. Serve at room temperature.

Spanakopita Is a Favorite Greek Comfort Food

Snack-sized spanakopita shaped into triangles or rolls is popular as mezze or an appetizer. Before you begin assembling the spanakopita, unroll the thawed phyllo sheets and place them carefully between two slightly damp kitchen cloths. This helps the sheets remain pliant so they won't tear too much. Organic phyllo is vegan and contains no preservatives, no cholesterol and no trans fat.

ASPARAGUS SALAD

ASPARAGUS
2 LBS FRESH ASPARAGUS, TRIMMED, BLANCHED AND CHILLED

VINAIGRETTE DRESSING
¼ C FINELY CHOPPED PARSLEY
2 T CHOPPED FRESH CHIVES
¼ C TARRAGON WHITE VINEGAR
2 T FINELY CHOPPED SHALLOTS
2 T MINCED SUNDRIED TOMATOES
1½ TSP DIJON MUSTARD
1½ TSP KOSHER SALT
FRESHLY GROUND PEPPER TO TASTE
½ C EXTRA VIRGIN OLIVE OIL

ASSEMBLE
2 SWEET RED PEPPERS, CHOPPED IN SMALL PIECES
2 YELLOW OR ORANGE PEPPERS, CHOPPED IN SMALL PIECES

Asparagus Blanch asparagus by placing it in boiling water for 3 minutes, then plunge immediately in ice water, then drain and chill.

Vinaigrette Dressing Combine first 8 ingredients and mix well. Let stand at room temperature for 30 minutes. Then add olive oil. This blends the flavors nicely.

Assemble Place chilled asparagus on a serving platter or salad plate, sprinkle on the two colors of peppers, then drizzle dressing on top.

Vegetables can be prepared one day ahead. Make dressing one day ahead, chill and bring to room temperature before serving.

Be sure to let the dressing mix stand for a while before adding the oil. It makes a big difference in the flavor.

MARITA'S CRANBERRY ORANGE BREAD PUDDING

- 4-5 CINNAMON CRUNCH BAGELS FROM PANERA, CUT INTO CUBES (ABOUT 10 CUPS)
- 3 C MILK
- 2 C ORANGE JUICE
- 5 EGGS
- 1½ C SUGAR
- ½ C BUTTER, MELTED
- 1 T VANILLA EXTRACT
- 1½ C CRAISINS (DRIED CRANBERRIES)
- 1 C CHOPPED PECANS
- 2 T ORANGE ZEST

Put bagel cubes into a large bowl. Combine milk, orange juice, eggs, sugar, butter and vanilla and mix into cubes. Let soak for 2-3 hours. Soaking time is very important.

Preheat oven to 350°F.

Stir in remaining ingredients and put into large 17x12-inch baking pan. Bake for 1 hour and 15 minutes until pudding is just set in the center.

Serves 24.

Jan Randle

Since I'm an avid reader, I collect cookbooks and recipes from anywhere and everywhere. And I study them. "What makes this recipe work?" I ask. "Why are there so many eggs in this cheesecake?" So, when we created this bread pudding in the testing kitchen, I had to ask questions. "What if someone doesn't live near a Panera store? What if Panera stops making Cinnamon Crunch Bagels? What if I don't need a recipe that serves 24 people?" Well, everybody adores this bread pudding, so I took on the job of answering the "What ifs?" Using different breads and pan sizes, I made this recipe four different times, with alterations. Here is what I found: This recipe can be divided in half (use 3 eggs, not 5), or you can bake it in two smaller pans and freeze one for later. Other kinds of bagels work well also, although if you use a plain bagel, add some cinnamon and sugar to the batter and sprinkle some on top. Other "sweet" bagels work well also, such as Cinnamon-Raisin. Oh, go ahead and make the full amount of Grand Marnier Sauce. You will want some extra.

GRAND MARNIER SAUCE

1 C HEAVY CREAM
¾ C PACKED BROWN SUGAR
½ C BUTTER
3 T GRAND MARNIER
1 TSP VANILLA EXTRACT
2 T ORANGE ZEST

Combine cream, brown sugar and butter in saucepan. Bring to boil and boil 5 minutes, stirring constantly. Remove from heat and stir in remaining ingredients. Spoon ½ of recipe over top of bread pudding before dishing up, then serve the rest on the side or on top of each serving.

125th Anniversary Celebration

CELEBRATION
CHAMPAGNE

COLD CUCUMBER
SCANDIA

STRAWBERRY AND
ROMAINE SALAD

THREE-CHEESE
SPINACH QUICHE

MOCHA GATEAU
WITH BUTTERCREAM
FROSTING

125TH ANNIVERSARY CELEBRATION
SEPTEMBER 15, 2016
CRESTVIEW COUNTRY CLUB GARDEN ROOM

It is an unusual day for the monthly Cooking Club meeting. A September meeting, to begin with, is a change. TACC has chosen to celebrate 125 years of existence a few months ahead of the actual anniversary date, which is December 3. The club was organized in 1891 and has been continually active all the years hence. Honorary members were invited to share the celebration. The tables were formally decorated with hydrangea centerpieces in the club colors of green and yellow, and ribbon-wrapped napkins.

Penny Moss

It was my privilege to serve as president of the cooking club during its 125th anniversary year. I helped plan the special luncheon for the occasion and wrote a "Brief History" booklet that was distributed that afternoon. In thinking of telling my story, I realized that my husband and I have been part of a couples' gourmet club for more than forty years! A group always coming up with interesting new foods, because everyone travels so much. The truth is that what I really love to make is beautiful and delicious desserts. Now that our children are grown, I don't make many desserts for myself and my husband.

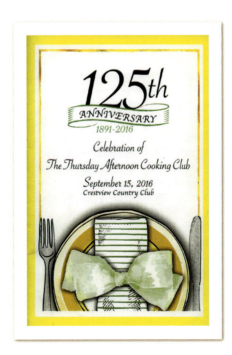

COLD CUCUMBER SCANDIA

3 MEDIUM CUCUMBERS
1 MEDIUM LEEK
2 T BUTTER
2 BAY LEAVES
1 T FLOUR
3 C CHICKEN BROTH
1 TSP SALT
1 C CREAM
JUICE OF 1 LEMON
SOUR CREAM
FRESH DILL, CHOPPED

Peel cucumbers. Slice 2 of them and sauté in butter with the bay leaves. Remove the dark green upper leaves on the leek and wash white part thoroughly. Slice thinly and sauté with cucumbers. Cook slowly until tender but not brown. Add flour and mix well. Add broth and salt. Simmer for 20-30 minutes. Press mixture through a sieve or use a ricer to remove whole seeds. Refrigerate until chilled.

Cut and seed the third cucumber, and dice finely before adding to chilled soup. Add cream, lemon juice and a bit of the chopped dill. Correct the seasoning. Serve in chilled glass cups with a dab of sour cream on top.

Serves 6.

Chilled Cucumber Soup is a wonderful recipe from the 1965 cookbook "A Treasury of Great Recipes" by Mary and Vincent Price. The original recipe came from the world-famous Scandia Restaurant on Sunset Strip in Los Angeles, California. Frank Sinatra and Marilyn Monroe ate at Scandia, and may just have sampled this recipe.

STRAWBERRY AND ROMAINE SALAD

SALAD
1 HEAD ROMAINE LETTUCE, WASHED AND TORN
1 PT FRESH STRAWBERRIES, SLICED
1 RED ONION, SLICED
¼ C SLIVERED ALMONDS, TOASTED

DRESSING
2 C MAYONNAISE
⅓ C SUGAR
⅓ C LIGHT CREAM
⅓ C RASPBERRY VINEGAR
2 T POPPY SEED
2-3 TSP RASPBERRY JAM

Combine dressing ingredients; set aside. Toss romaine, strawberries and onion. Just before serving, drizzle dressing over salad. Garnish with almonds.

Serves 8.

THREE-CHEESE SPINACH QUICHE

CRUST FOR 9-INCH PIE OR FROZEN PUFF PASTRY CRUST
1 (10-OZ) PACKAGE FROZEN CHOPPED SPINACH, THAWED
½ C FINELY CHOPPED ONION
1 C WHIPPING CREAM
¼ TSP SALT
½ TSP PEPPER
3 LARGE EGGS, LIGHTLY BEATEN
2 C (8-10 OZ) SHREDDED MOZZARELLA CHEESE – DIVIDED USE
½ C (2 OZ) SHREDDED CHEDDAR CHEESE
1 (7-OZ) JAR ROASTED RED PEPPERS, DRAINED AND CHOPPED
½ C (2 OZ) CRUMBLED FETA CHEESE

This recipe was a winner in a "Taste of Home, Test Kitchen" submission. "Tasteofhome.com" features recipes from home cooks which have passed the test of repeated use.

Red and green rise to the top of this creamy quiche. Prepare your crust of choice and bake as directed. Let cool on a wire rack. Preheat oven to 350°F.

Thaw spinach thoroughly and squeeze until very dry. (Roll it up in a dish towel and squeeze repeatedly.) Cook onion in a splash of olive oil until translucent. Combine ½ cup mozzarella cheese, spinach, onion, cream, salt, pepper and eggs, stirring well. Sprinkle 1½ cups mozzarella and cheddar cheese into pastry shell. Add spinach mixture. Top with red pepper; sprinkle with feta cheese. Bake, uncovered at 350°F for 1 hour or until set. Cover loosely with aluminum foil and let stand 30 minutes before serving.

Yield one 9" quiche.

Quiche that turns out to be mostly eggy turns people off quiche of any flavor. This quiche with its three cheeses and veggies is outstandingly delicious. If you are using puff pastry, freeze it at least 15 minutes before filling to make the pastry firmer.

MOCHA GATEAU
WITH BUTTERCREAM FROSTING

GENOISE CAKE
1 T INSTANT ESPRESSO POWDER
1 T UNSWEETENED COCOA POWDER
3 T HOT WATER
1 T COFFEE FLAVORED LIQUEUR
1 T CHOCOLATE, MELTED
1 C SIFTED CAKE FLOUR
1½ TSP BAKING POWDER
¼ TSP SALT
3 EGG WHITES
3 EG YOLKS
1 C WHITE SUGAR

MOCHA BUTTERCREAM FROSTING
1½ C BUTTER, SOFTENED
3 C POWDERED SUGAR
4 T COCOA POWDER
2 TSP VANILLA EXTRACT
2 TSP INSTANT COFFEE DISSOLVED
    IN A SPLASH OF HOT WATER

GANACHE
3 OZ DARK CHOCOLATE
3 OZ HEAVY WHIPPING CREAM

Preheat oven to 250°F. Grease and lightly flour two 9-inch cake pans. Dissolve the espresso and cocoa powders in the hot water, set aside.

Cake In a large mixing bowl, whip egg whites to soft peaks. Gradually sprinkle in ¼ cup sugar while continuing to whip until stiff but not dry. In a separate bowl whip egg yolks with remaining sugar until thick and pale, about 5 minutes. Stir in the espresso mixture, then stir in the flour, baking powder and salt. Gently stir until incorporated. Fold ⅓ of the egg whites into the batter until very well mixed, then gently fold in the remaining egg whites. Divide the batter between the two pans and spread evenly. Bake 25-30 minutes until the top springs back when lightly pressed.

Frosting In your mixer, beat the softened butter with the powdered sugar until it is creamy. Add the cocoa powder, vanilla and coffee. Beat with the mixer until it is nice and fluffy (about 2 minutes).

Ganache Finely chop chocolate and place into a bowl. Bring cream to just barely a simmer and pour over chocolate. Cover and let stand 2 minutes. Stir until combined and smooth. Allow to cool and thicken before using on cake.

Assembly Spread half of the frosting on one layer of the cake. Add the second layer and spread the remaining frosting very smoothly on top and around the side. Refrigerate for at least 3 hours before adding the ganache. Using a small spoon, place dollops of ganache around the top edges of the cake, allowing some to drip down. Fill in the top of the cake with more ganache and spread with an offset spatula.

Serves 12.

21

TINY TREASURES
POTS DE CRÈME

HOW TO MAKE POTS DE CRÈME

BUTTERSCOTCH POTS DE CRÈME
with Salted Caramel and Crème Fraîche

CHAMBORD ESPRESSO POTS DE CRÈME
with Chocolate

STRAWBERRY POTS DE CRÈME

WHITE CHOCOLATE POTS DE CRÈME

BITTERSWEET CHOCOLATE
POTS DE CRÈME

SALTED CARAMEL POTS DE CRÈME

CHOCOLATE-HAZELNUT MERINGUES

HOW TO MAKE POTS DE CRÈME

Pots de Crème is a French dessert custard dating to the 17th century. The name means "pot of custard" or "pot of cream," and also refers to the porcelain cups in which the dessert is served.

The Thursday Afternoon Cooking Club has enjoyed serving Pots de Crème since its very early days. The tiny desserts come in many flavors and are so rich they are served in small – but satisfying – amounts. The very first TACC minute book refers to cups of chocolate served for dessert on December 12, 1892.

These tiny desserts were enjoyed from time to time by the club, until in 1997, the husband of Sally Cardwell, a former member, donated 18 Mottahedeh pots de crème cups to the club in her memory. These little cups are treasured for their association with a departed friend. Many members have also acquired their own varied sets. The following recipes reflect the extensive variety of flavors served by club members.

For 90 years, Mottahedeh has been a recognized leader in luxury ceramic antique reproductions and historic designs. The photo at right shows Mottahedeh pots de crème cups with butterscotch custard.

Notes on Pots de Crème

1. If you don't have official pots de crème, use custard cups or espresso cups.

2. Don't use a stand mixer; bubbles are the enemy. Whisk by hand.

3. You may decide whether or not to filter the mixture based on your own acceptance of a bit of chocolate or strawberry seeds in the completed dessert.

4. If you line the bottom of the baking pan with a kitchen towel, the cups won't slide around.

5. Always bake pots in a water bath that comes about halfway up the cups. Cover with foil.

6. Custards are done when slightly set at the edges and still wobbly in the center.

7. Let the pots stand in the hot water after baking for about 10 minutes. Then refrigerate.

8. Custards wrapped in plastic can be stored in the refrigerator for up to 2 weeks.

Chris Kubik

I love to make and eat Pots de Crème. Butterscotch Pots de Crème is my current favorite. I first tasted it on vacation at Big Horn Fishing Lodge in Montana, where the chef agreed to share the recipe. I have served it to cooking club and bridge club and couples cooking club to absolute raves every time. Pots de crème, any flavor, is a perfect dessert because of its small amount and intensity of flavor.

This recipe was discovered by Chris Kubik in a cookbook by talented chef Travis Lett. Lett's restaurant, Gielina, is currently one of Los Angeles' most-talked-about restaurants.

BUTTERSCOTCH POTS DE CRÈME
WITH SALTED CARAMEL AND CRÈME FRAÎCHE

BUTTERSCOTCH CUSTARD
9 EGG YOLKS, AT ROOM TEMPERATURE
1¼ C PACKED DARK BROWN SUGAR
4 T UNSALTED BUTTER
3½ C HEAVY CREAM
1 TSP KOSHER SALT
½ VANILLA BEAN, SPLIT LENGTHWISE

CARAMEL SAUCE
¼ C GRANULATED SUGAR
2¼ TSP WATER
¼ TSP KOSHER SALT
⅓ C HEAVY CREAM
¼ C WHIPPING CREAM

BUTTERMILK CRÈME FRAÎCHE
4 C HEAVY CREAM
1 T BUTTERMILK (OR PURCHASED CRÈME FRAÎCHE)

Preheat the oven to 300°F. Arrange eight custard pots with a ¾-cup capacity in a large, shallow baking pan. Set a fine-mesh sieve over a large liquid measuring cup or pitcher. Place the egg yolks in a large bowl and set aside.

Custard In a medium, heavy-bottomed saucepan over medium heat, cook the brown sugar and butter, without stirring, until the sugar turns a deep amber color and develops a nutty smell, 10 to 15 minutes. Pour the heavy cream into the mixture gradually, whisking constantly. Remove from the heat. Add the kosher salt, and scrape the seeds from the vanilla bean into the mixture. Stir to combine. Slowly pour the hot butterscotch mixture into the egg yolks, whisking constantly. Strain the custard into the measuring cup. Pour into ramekins, dividing the custard evenly. Bake for 45 minutes. Rotate the pan and continue to bake for 15 minutes more. Remove from the oven and set on a cooling rack. The custards can be made up to 1 week in advance and stored, covered, in the refrigerator.

Caramel Sauce In a small saucepan over medium-high heat, combine the granulated sugar, water and kosher salt and cook, without stirring, until the mixture turns red-brown in color, about 5 minutes. Gradually add the heavy cream, whisking constantly until the sauce is smooth. Set aside.

Buttermilk Crème Fraîche In a 1-quart jar, combine the cream and buttermilk. Partially cover and let stand in a warm spot (about 78°F) until the cream tastes slightly sour and has thickened to a pudding-like consistency.

CHAMBORD ESPRESSO POTS DE CRÈME
WITH CHOCOLATE

½ C CHAMBORD LIQUEUR
1 T ESPRESSO POWDER
3 T SUGAR
6 OZ SEMISWEET CHOCOLATE, CHOPPED
1½ C HEAVY CREAM
¾ C WHOLE MILK
7 LARGE EGG YOLKS

Preheat the oven to 300°F. Place oven rack in middle position.

Mix Chambord, espresso and 1 tablespoon sugar. Put mixture in a pan and cook over medium heat, stirring constantly without stopping until mixture is reduced by half. Allow to cool. In a medium pan, scald cream and milk, and remove pan from heat. Add chocolate and stir until melted and smooth. Allow to cool. Add Chambord mixture.

Working in a bowl, whisk yolks with remaining 2 tablespoons sugar until mixture is pale and thick. Very gradually and gently, whisk liquid into egg mixture, being careful not to create air bubbles.

Arrange cups in a small roasting pan. Fill each cup to the top with custard mixture. Bake about 40 minutes. Pots de Crème can be prepared ahead and stored in the refrigerator. Serve at room temperature.

Similar recipes call for ¾ cup of sugar, so if you want it sweeter, add sugar.

Serves 8.

STRAWBERRY POTS DE CRÈME

2 C HEAVY CREAM
½ C STRAWBERRY PUREE, STRAINED
½ C SUGAR
5 EGG YOLKS
PINK FOOD COLORING
TOPPINGS: STRAWBERRIES

Preheat oven to 300°F and place a rack in the center of oven.

In a small saucepan over medium-low heat, combine cream, strawberry puree and ¼ cup sugar and bring slowly to a simmer. In a large bowl whisk the eggs and remaining sugar until well combined. Slowly whisk a small amount of the cream mixture into the yolks to temper them. Continue adding the warm cream very slowly, continuing to whisk until all of it has been added. Add pink coloring if desired.

Place ramekins in a 9x13-inch baking dish and pour custard evenly into them. Bake for 45-55 minutes.

Remove molds from hot water and place on a cooling rack to let cool. Then refrigerate for 8 hours or overnight before topping with additional strawberries.

Serves 6.

Paired with a couple of dark chocolate truffles, this gorgeous pot de crème is completely irresistible. The bright pink color whispers springtime, and the dash of whipped cream announces incomparable richness. Try this. You'll be so glad you did.

WHITE CHOCOLATE POTS DE CRÈME

4 OZ WHITE CHOCOLATE, CHOPPED
6 LARGE EGG YOLKS
½ C SUGAR
3 C HEAVY WHIPPING CREAM
1-INCH X 3-INCH STRIP LEMON PEEL
½ TSP VANILLA EXTRACT
FRESH BERRIES AND WHIPPED CREAM
8 5-OZ CUPS OR RAMEKINS

Preheat oven to 300°F.

Custard Put egg yolks in a medium mixing bowl and whisk; add sugar and whisk until combined. Set aside.

Put cream and lemon peel into a heavy sauce pot. Scald the mixture over medium-high heat. Put the white chocolate in a small bowl and pour hot cream over, whisking to melt chocolate.

Gradually whisk the cream into the egg mixture, add vanilla, and whisk to combine.

Pour into cups and place in a baking pan. Bake for about 35-45 minutes. Custards are done when edges are set but centers are slightly shaky.

Remove from water, cool and refrigerate several hours or overnight.

Serve with a dollop of softly whipped cream and a few berries.

Serves 8.

BITTERSWEET CHOCOLATE POTS DE CRÈME

1 C HEAVY CREAM
¾ C WHOLE MILK
⅓ C SUGAR
4 OZ BITTERSWEET CHOCOLATE, CHOPPED
1 T UNSWEETENED COCOA POWDER
1 TSP VANILLA EXTRACT
1 TSP CHOCOLATE EXTRACT OR KAHLÚA LIQUEUR
⅛ TSP SALT
6 EGG YOLKS

GARNISH
WHIPPED CREAM, WHITE CHOCOLATE CURLS, ALMONDS OR RASPBERRIES

Preheat oven to 275°F.

Custard In a medium saucepan, combine cream, milk, sugar, chocolate, cocoa powder, vanilla extract, chocolate extract and salt. Cook over medium-high heat, stirring constantly until the mixture just begins to boil; remove from heat.

In a medium bowl, whisk the egg yolks until smooth. Very gradually, add hot mixture to egg yolks, whisking constantly. Strain mixture through a fine-mesh sieve.

Evenly divide the mixture among 6 pot de crème cups, and set them in an ovenproof pan. Cover with foil and bake approximately 45 minutes, or until set around the edges, but still wobbly in the centers.

Remove the pan from the oven and remove foil. Let pots cool in the pan for 30 minutes. Refrigerate 4 hours before serving. Garnish with whipped cream, white chocolate curls, almonds or raspberries, if desired.

Serves 6.

Easy White Chocolate Curls

Soften white chocolate slightly in microwave oven (about 30 seconds for 1 square). Holding square within a paper towel, draw a vegetable peeler across edge of square, allowing curls to drop to a piece of waxed paper. When done, place in refrigerator until curls are set. Transfer to dessert when hardened.

SALTED CARAMEL POTS DE CRÈME

4 T (½ STICK) UNSALTED BUTTER
¾ C PACKED LIGHT BROWN SUGAR
½ TSP KOSHER SALT
½ VANILLA BEAN,
  SPLIT LENGTHWISE
1¾ C HEAVY CREAM
¾ C WHOLE MILK
6 LARGE EGG YOLKS
FLAKE SEA SALT, SUCH AS MALDON,
  FOR GARNISH

Custard In a large heavy saucepan, melt the butter over medium heat. Whisk in the brown sugar and kosher salt. Using the tip of a small sharp knife, scrape the vanilla seeds from the bean, add to the butter mixture, and drop in the bean. Stir for about 5 minutes, or until the mixture has the texture of thick sand, and has taken on a nutty, caramel fragrance. Reduce the heat to medium-low and gradually whisk in the cream. The mixture will bubble vigorously and will seize when the cream is added. Whisk for about 5 minutes, or until the hardened sugar bits dissolve and the mixture begins to boil. Remove the pan from the heat and whisk in the milk. Remove vanilla bean.

In a large bowl, stir the egg yolks to blend. Gradually whisk in the warm caramel mixture. Strain the custard into a large liquid measuring cup. Pour the custard into the cups, dividing it equally.

Bake Preheat oven to 325°F. Position a rack in the center of the oven. Place eight ½-cup ramekins (4-ounce) or cups, in a large baking pan.

The baking pan should have hot water about halfway up the sides of the cups, and be covered with aluminum foil. Bake the custards for about 50 minutes, or until they are just set around the edges but still jiggle slightly when the cups are gently shaken. Remove the cups from the pan and transfer to a wire rack to cool, about 1 hour. Cover with plastic wrap and refrigerate at least 4 hours, or up to 2 days.

Serve At the last minute, sprinkle a pinch of sea salt over each pot de crème and serve chilled.

Serves 8.

CHOCOLATE-HAZELNUT MERINGUES

5 LARGE EGG WHITES
½ TSP CREAM OF TARTAR
⅛ TSP SALT
½ C GRANULATED SUGAR
½ C PACKED BROWN SUGAR
1 TSP VANLLA EXTRACT
3 OZ SEMISWEET CHOCOLATE
⅓ C BLANCHED WHOLE HAZELNUTS, TOASTED AND FINELY CHOPPED (OR USE PECANS)

Cooking Light recipe by David Bonom.

Preheat oven to 250°F.

Place egg whites in a large bowl; beat with a mixer at high speed until foamy. Add cream of tartar and salt, beating until soft peaks form. Gradually add sugars, 1 tablespoon at a time, beating until stiff peaks form. Add vanilla; beat 1 minute.

Cover 2 baking sheets with parchment paper. Spoon 24 (2-inch-round) mounds onto prepared baking sheets. Place in oven; bake 1 hour or until dry to touch, rotating pans halfway through cooking. (Meringues are done when surface is dry and meringues can be removed from paper without sticking to fingers.)

Turn oven off. Cool meringues in oven 1 hour. Remove from oven; carefully remove meringues from paper.

Place chocolate in a medium glass bowl. Microwave on high 1 minute or until almost melted, stirring until smooth.

Dip side of each meringue in melted chocolate and chopped hazelnuts.

Yield 12 servings (serving size: 2 meringues).

INDEX

Accompaniments
- Basil and Cilantro, Cheese and Shrimp Stuffed Poblanos — 130
- Cherry Preserves, Brambles — 51
- Flake Sea Salt, Salted Carmel Pots de Crème — 223
- Pepperoncini, Quick Italian Salad — 163
- Pumpkin Seeds, Chicken Pot Pies — 176

Almonds
- Almond Cookies — 146
- Spanish Almond Flan — 137

Apples
- Apple Cake with Caramel Sauce — 164
- Apple, Cheddar, Spiced Pecan Salad — 115
- Apple Cider, Chicken Pot Pies — 176
- Apple Cranberry Muffins — 116

Artichokes
- Baked Crab Croissant, Artichokes — 96

Asparagus
- Asparagus Salad — 195
- Roasted Shrimp and Orzo — 112

Avocados
- Avocado-Cucumber Soup — 141
- Fiesta Chicken Salad — 142
- Mexican Chopped Salad, Avocado — 133

Beans
- Mexican Chopped Salad, Black Beans — 133

Beef
- Ground Beef, Eggplant Yukhnee — 80

Beets
- Beet, Romaine and Goat Cheese Salad — 168
- Golden Beet, Farro and Watercress Salad — 153

Bell Peppers
- Green Peppers, Sausage Corn Chowder — 170
- Red and Orange Peppers, Asparagus Salad — 195
- Red Bell Pepper Sauce — 130
- Red and Yellow Peppers, Fiesta Chicken Salad — 142

Breads
- Apple Cranberry Muffins — 116
- Baguette with Za'atar — 84
- Baked Crab Croissant — 96
- Caraway Puffs — 125
- Cheddar Buttermilk Corn Bread — 134
- Cinnamon Crunch Bagels, Bread Pudding — 196
- Delicious Corn Bread — 27
- No-Knead Dutch-Oven Crusty Bread — 171
- Orange Muffins, Tiny — 145
- Parmesan Toast — 163
- Potato Split Biscuit — 49

Buttermilk
- Buttermilk Crème Fraîche — 213
- Cheddar Buttermilk Corn Bread — 134
- Dill Sauce — 150
- Orange Muffins, Tiny — 145
- Southwestern Corn Bread Pudding — 134

Cakes
- Angel Food Cake — 23
- Apple Cake with Caramel Sauce — 164
- Carrot Cake, The Prospect's — 118
- Mocha Gateau with Buttercream Frosting — 207
- Molten Chocolate Cakes with Grandmother Sauce — 189
- Semolina Honey Lemon Syrup Cake — 87
- Triple Chocolate Mousse Cake — 154
- Wichita Cake — 31

Casseroles
- Southwestern Corn Bread Pudding — 134

Cheese
- Apple, Cheddar, Spiced Pecan Salad — 115
- Cotija, Mexican Chopped Salad — 133
- Goat Cheese, Gorgonzola, Romaine, Beet Salad — 168

Gorgonzola, Feta, Roasted Pear Salad	106
Mascarpone, White Crème	146
Monterey Jack, Baked Crab Croissant	96
Monterey Jack, Cheese and Shrimp Stuffed Poblanos	130
Monterey Jack, Sausage Corn Chowder	170
Mozzarella, Italian Lasagna Torte	160
Three-Cheese Spinach Quiche	204
Velveeta, Georgia's Cheese Soufflé	90

Cheese, Blue
Fruit and Blue Cheese Salad	124

Cheese, Cheddar
Baked Crab Croissant	96
Cheddar Buttermilk Corn Bread	134

Cheese, Cottage
Caraway Puffs with Cottage Cheese	125

Cheese, Cream
Coconut Cream Cheese Frosting	118
Pumpkin Cheesecake	173

Cheese, Feta
Fiesta Chicken Salad	142
Spanakopita, Spinach Pie	192

Cheese, Goat
Beet, Romaine and Goat Cheese Salad	168
Cheese and Shrimp Stuffed Poblanos	130

Chicken
Chicken Pot Pie with Phyllo	176
Crab-Stuffed Chicken	122
Fiesta Chicken Salad	142

Chili, Chilies
Poblanos, Serrano or Jalapeño, Cheese and Shrimp Stuffed Poblanos	130

Chocolate
Bittersweet Chocolate Pots de Crème	220
Chambord Espresso Chocolate Pots de Crème	215
Chocolate Hazelnut Meringues	224
Chocolate Leaves	157
Chocolate Marshmallow Pie	92
Chocolate Whipped Cream Icing, Angel Food Cake	23
Mocha Gateau with Buttercream Frosting	207
Molten Chocolate Cakes	189
No-Cook Chocolate Mocha Ice Cream	108
S'Mores Coffee and Fudge Ice Cream Cake	100
Triple Chocolate Mousse Cake	154
White Chocolate Pots de Crème	219

Coconut
Coconut Cream Cheese Frosting	118

Condensed Milk
Spanish Almond Flan	137

Condiments
Capers, Dill, Wasabi Marinade, Roasted Salmon	150

Cookies
Almond Cookies	146
Brambles	51
Chocolate-Hazelnut Meringues	224
Gingersnap Cookies, Pumpkin Cheesecake	173
Grandma Pearl's Ice Box Cookies	109

Corn
Fiesta Chicken Salad	142
Frozen Corn, Mexican Chopped Salad	133
Sausage Corn Chowder	170
Southwestern Corn Bread Pudding	134

Corn Meal
Cheddar Buttermilk Corn Bread	134
Delicious Corn Bread	27

INDEX

Crab Meat
    Crab-Stuffed Chicken   122
    Open-Faced Baked Crab Croissant   96
    Shellfish Crepes in Wine-Cheese Sauce   105

Craisins
    Cranberry Orange Bread Pudding   196

Cranberries
    Apple Cranberry Muffins   116
    Cranberry Salad with
        Raspberry Jell-O   91

Crepes
    Shellfish Crepes in Wine-Cheese Sauce   105

Cucumbers
    Avocado-Cucumber Soup   141
    Cucumber Scandia   202

Custard
    Bittersweet Chocolate Pots de Crème   220
    Butterscotch Pots de Crème   213
    Chambord Espresso Chocolate
        Pots de Crème   215
    Crème Brule with Brownie Bottom   180
    Salted Caramel Pots de Crème   223
    Spanish Almond Flan   137
    Strawberry Pots de Crème   216
    White Chocolate Pots de Crème   219

Desserts
    Angel Food Cake   23
    Angel Pie   37
    Apple Cake with Caramel Sauce   164
    Brownie-Bottom Crème Brule   180
    Brownies   180
    Butter Pecan Pumpkin Pie   127
    Chocolate Marshmallow Pie   92
    Cranberry Orange Bread Pudding   196
    Eggnog Ice Cream   108
    Flan, Spanish Almond   137
    Ganache   207
    Mocha Gateau with
        Buttercream Frosting   207
    Molten Chocolate Cakes   189
    No-Cook Chocolate Mocha Ice Cream   108
    Semolina Honey Lemon Syrup Cake   87
    S'Mores Coffee and Fudge Ice Cream Cake   100
    Strawberry Mousse   49
    Triple Chocolate Mousse Cake   154
    White Crème   146
    Wichita Cake   31

Dill
    Dill, Capers and Wasabi Marinade   150
    Dill Sauce   150

Edamame
    Mexican Chopped Salad, Edamame   133

Egg Dishes
    Good Friday Eggs   49
    Three-Cheese Spinach Quiche   204

Egg Whites
    Angel Pie   37
    Chocolate-Hazelnut Meringues   224

Egg Yolks
    Bittersweet Chocolate Pots de Crème   220
    Butterscotch Pots de Crème   213
    Chambord Espresso Chocolate
        Pots de Crème   215
    Salted Caramel Pots de Crème   223
    Strawberry Pots de Crème   216
    White Chocolate Pots de Crème   219

Eggplant
    Eggplant Yukhnee   80

Entrees
    Autumn Chicken Pot Pies with Phyllo   176
    Beet, Farro and Watercress Salad   153
    Cheese and Shrimp Stuffed Poblano Chilies   130

Cider-Roasted Pork Tenderloin	184
Crab-Stuffed Chicken	122
Eggplant Yukhnee	80
Fiesta Chicken Salad	142
Georgia's Cheese Soufflé	90
Northern Italian Lasagna Torte	160
Open-Faced Baked Crab Croissant	96
Roasted Salmon	150
Roasted Shrimp and Orzo	112
Sausage Corn Chowder	170
Shellfish Crepes in Wine-Cheese Sauce	105
Spanakopita, Spinach Pie	192
Three-Cheese Spinach Quiche	204

Fish

Cheese and Shrimp Stuffed Poblanos	130
Crab-Stuffed Chicken	122
Open-Faced Baked Crab Croissant	96
Roasted Salmon	150
Roasted Shrimp and Orzo	112
Shellfish Crepes in Wine-Cheese Sauce	105

Frostings, Glazes, Toppings

Chocolate Whipped Cream Icing, Angel Food Cake	23
Coconut Cream Cheese Frosting	118
Mocha Buttercream Frosting	207

Fruit (See individual kinds)

Citrus and Pomegranate Salad	83
Festive Fresh Fruit Salad, Mangos, Pears, Grapes	179
Fruit and Blue Cheese Salad	124
Roasted Pear Salad	106
Strawberry and Romaine Salad	203
Strawberry Pots de Crème	216
White Crème with Strawberries	146

Grains

Beet, Farro and Watercress Salad	153

Ground Beef

Eggplant Yukhnee	80

Ice Cream

Butter Pecan (Ice Cream) Pumpkin Pie	127
Eggnog Ice Cream	108
No-Cook Chocolate Mocha Ice Cream	108
S'Mores Coffee and Fudge Ice Cream Cake	100

Jell-O

Cranberry Salad, Raspberry Jell-O	91
Perfection Salad	34

Lemon

Angel Pie	37

Lettuce

Arugula, Romaine, Beet Salad	168
Iceberg, Quick Italian	163
Romaine, Beet and Goat Cheese Salad	168
Strawberry and Romaine Salad	203

Marinades

Dill, Capers and Wasabi Marinade	150

Marshmallows

Chocolate Marshmallow Pie	92
S'Mores Coffee and Fudge Ice Cream Cake	100

Meringue

Angel Pie	37

Nuts

Apple, Cheddar, Spiced Pecan Salad	115
Apple Cranberry Muffins, Walnuts	116
Candied Pecans	106
Glazed Walnuts	186
Toasted Pistachios	168

Onions

Cipollini Onions, Roasted Pork Tenderloin	184

Orange

Citrus and Pomegranate Salad	83
Orange Muffins, Tiny	145

INDEX

Pasta
- Lebanese Rice — 84
- Northern Italian Lasagne Torte — 160
- Roasted Shrimp and Orzo — 112

Pear
- Roasted Pear Salad,
    Apple-Grape Vinaigrette — 106

Peas
- Chicken Pot Pies with Phyllo — 176

Peppers
- Poblano Pepper, Cheese and Shrimp
    Stuffed Poblanos — 130
- Red Bell, Cheese and Shrimp
    Stuffed Poblanos — 130
- Serrano or Jalapeño, Cheese and Shrimp
    Stuffed Poblanos — 130

Phyllo Pastry
- Autumn Chicken Pot Pies
    with Phyllo — 176
- Spanakopita, Spinach Pie — 192

Pies, Pastries
- Angel Pie — 37
- Butter Pecan Pumpkin Pie — 127
- Chocolate Marshmallow Pie — 92
- Savory Pinwheels — 157
- Spanakopita, Spinach Pie — 192

Pomegranate
- Pomegranate and Citrus Salad — 83

Poppy Seed
- Poppy Seed Dressing — 203

Pork
- Italian Sausage, Lasagna Torte — 160
- Pancetta, Roasted Pork Tenderloin — 184
- Pork Sausage Corn Chowder — 170
- Roasted Pork Tenderloin
    With Calvados Cream Sauce — 184

Potatoes
- Garlic Parmesan Roasted Potatoes — 185

Pots de Crème
- Bittersweet Chocolate — 220
- Butterscotch with Salted Caramel
    and Crème Fraîche — 213
- Chambord Chocolate and Espresso — 215
- How to Make Pots de Crème — 210
- Salted Caramel — 223
- Strawberry — 216
- White Chocolate — 219

Pumpkin
- Butter Pecan Pumpkin Pie — 127
- Pumpkin Cheesecake, Mooselips — 173

Quiche
- Three-Cheese Spinach Quiche — 204

Raisins
- Golden, Tiny Orange Muffins — 145
- Wichita Cake — 31

Rice
- Lebanese Rice — 84

Salad Dressings
- Apple Cider Vinegar Dressing — 115
- Apple-Grape Vinaigrette — 106
- Balsamic Italian Dressing — 186
- Citrus and Spice Vinaigrette,
    Cumin, Coriander — 133
- Easy Dressing — 83
- Fig Vinaigrette — 153
- Lime Cilantro Vinaigrette — 142
- Mustard Poppy Seed Dressing — 124
- Orange Amaretto Sauce — 179
- Parmesan Dressing — 163
- Poppy Seed Raspberry Dressing — 203
- Raspberry Dressing — 168
- Vinaigrette Dressing — 195

Salads
- Asparagus Salad — 195
- Beet, Farro and Watercress Salad — 153
- Citrus and Pomegranate Salad — 83
- Cranberry Salad — 91
- Fall Salad with Italian Dressing — 186
- Festive Fresh Fruit Salad — 179
- Fruit and Blue Cheese Salad — 124
- Mexican Chopped Salad — 133
- Quick Italian Salad — 163
- Strawberry and Romaine Salad — 203
- Tomato Aspic Salad — 99

Salads, Main Dish
- Beet, Farro and Watercress Salad — 153
- Fiesta Chicken Salad — 142

Salmon
- Roasted Salmon — 150

Sandwiches
- Open-Faced Baked Crab Croissant — 96

Sauces, Savory
- Hollandaise Sauce — 122
- Lasagne Red Sauce — 160
- Lasagna White Sauce — 160
- Red Bell Pepper Sauce — 130
- Wine-Cheese Sauce — 105

Sauces, Sweet
- Caramel Sauce, Butterscotch Pots de Crème — 213
- Caramel Sauce, Italian Apple Cake — 164
- Caramel Swirl Topping — 173
- Fudge Sauce — 100
- Grand Marnier Sauce — 197
- Grandmother Sauce — 189
- Honey-Lemon Syrup — 87

Sausage
- Sausage Corn Chowder — 170
- Italian Sausage, Lasagna — 160

Shrimp
- Cheese and Shrimp Stuffed Poblanos — 130

Soups, Cold
- Avocado-Cucumber Soup — 141
- Cucumber Scandia — 202

Soups, Hot
- Sausage Corn Chowder — 170

Spices
- Caraway Puffs — 125
- Cumin, Sausage Corn Chowder — 170
- Ginger, Pumpkin Cheesecake — 173
- Lebanese Spice or Allspice — 80
- Wasabi, Dill Capers, Roasted Salmon — 150
- Za'atar Spice Blend — 84

Spinach
- Spanakopita, Spinach Pie — 192
- Three-Cheese Spinach Quiche — 204

Squash
- Butternut Squash, Chicken Pot Pies — 176

Strawberries
- Strawberry and Romaine Salad — 203
- Strawberry Pots de Crème — 216
- White Crème with Strawberries — 146

Tomatoes
- Cherry, Avocado-Cucumber Soup — 141
- Eggplant Yukhnee — 80
- Italian Tomatoes, 28-oz can — 160
- Mexican Chopped Salad, Grape Tomatoes — 133
- Roma, Fiesta Chicken Salad — 142
- Tomato Aspic Salad — 99

Vegetables (See individual kinds)